Quick to Stitch
CROSS STITCH
KEEPSAKES

HELEN PHILIPPS

David and Charles

A DAVID & CHARLES BOOK
Copyright © David & Charles Limited 2008

David & Charles is an F+W Publications Inc. company
4700 East Galbraith Road Cincinnati, OH 45236

First published in the UK in 2008

Text, artworks and designs copyright © Helen Philipps 2008
Photography and diagrams copyright © David & Charles 2008

A catalogue record for this book is available from the British Library.

ISBN-13: 978-0-7153-2747-0 hardback
ISBN-10: 0-7153-2747-X hardback

ISBN-13: 978-0-7153-2752-4 paperback
ISBN-10: 0-7153-2752-6 paperback

Printed in China by SNP Leefung
for David & Charles
Brunel House   Newton Abbot   Devon

Executive Editor Cheryl Brown
Desk Editor Bethany Dymond
Project Editor and Chart Preparation Lin Clements
Senior Designer Charly Bailey
Designer Mia Farrant
Production Controller Ros Napper

Visit our website at www.davidandcharles.co.uk

David & Charles books are available from all good bookshops;
alternatively you can contact our Orderline on 0870 9908222 or
write to us at FREEPOST EX2 110, D&C Direct, Newton Abbot, TQ12 4ZZ
(no stamp required UK only); US customers call 800-289-0963
and Canadian customers call 800-840-5220.

To my husband David
with all my love

Contents

INTRODUCTION

It is always a delightful treat to receive a handmade gift, and a great way to show appreciation and affection to valued friends and loved ones is to spend time making them a keepsake, something personal they will value for many years. It is also very soothing to take time from the bustle of our busy lives to quietly stitch a small project that will not take too long to complete.

This book is packed with projects to create gorgeous gifts and treats for you, your family and friends of all ages. The book will spark your own creativity too, as it contains many suggestions for other ways you could use the charted motifs, alphabets and numerals provided.

There are 20 lovely samplers to stitch and record many of life's celebrations and milestones, including a selection of sweet mini samplers too – ideal for when time is really short. There is also an extensive collection of smaller gifts and keepsakes – some of which are previewed overleaf – perfect to give to your loved ones and show them just how much you care. With 200 charted designs to choose from you are sure to find something to stitch all year long and create some wonderful memories along the way.

How This Book Works

♥ Every chapter features a showcase sampler with full stitching instructions, plus many smaller designs with shorter instructions, all made up in different ways (see some examples overleaf).

♥ Each chapter has its charted designs within the chapter, some of which have been made up into projects.

♥ The charted designs are very versatile and there are ideas in each chapter suggesting different ways to use the designs, so look out for these 'Craft a Keepsake' features.

♥ Each page of charted motifs has a key, which also gives the number of strands of thread to use for the various stitches. Check what colours a motif uses before you buy threads.

♥ Arrows have been included on most charted motifs to help you find the centre. If you need help, refer to page 90 for working out stitch count and finished design sizes.

♥ The majority of making up instructions are at the back of the book beginning on page 94. See page 90 for materials and techniques needed and page 92 for instructions on working the stitches.

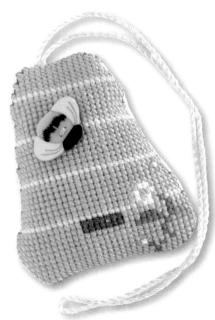

The book features 20 small, contemporary sampler designs perfect for celebrating the big occasions in life. The Friends Sampler shown right is simple to stitch but makes a lasting impression. Making a smaller gift, such as the Beehive Scissor Keeper above, is a quick and charming way to send good wishes.

CRAFTING KEEPSAKES

These two pages give you a sneak preview of some of the lovely projects featured in the book, providing you with a wealth of ideas for attractive, contemporary cards, gifts and keepsakes. These innovative ideas are perfect to stitch as reminders of good times, good friends or good deeds. The designs charted throughout the chapters have been created to be highly versatile, so you can use them on a wide range of project ideas. Look through the book for the designs you like and make gifts as unique as the people you are stitching them for.

Cross stitch works beautifully with beads and many of the projects are embellished with shiny seed beads. This beautiful keepsake heart uses beads instead of cross stitches in part of the design, while larger beads are used to create a luxurious tassel.

The smallest cross stitch motif can be transformed into the sweetest keepsake and this stuffed star could be hung from a cot or pram. You could change the shape to a heart and stitch the message of your choice or a child's name.

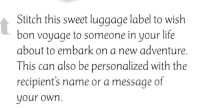

Stitch this sweet luggage label to wish bon voyage to someone in your life about to embark on a new adventure. This can also be personalized with the recipient's name or a message of your own.

Cross stitch embroideries are wonderful for decorating bags, as this delightful little creation shows, and the big buttons add a lovely finishing touch. The stitching is easily fused to the fabric with iron-on adhesive webbing. Instead of a single letter, you could stitch the recipient's name or create a message using one of the charted alphabets.

Making cards is probably the quickest way to use the designs in this book and there are literally hundreds of motifs to choose from, including gift tag ideas. Mount the stitching in a ready-made card or make your own – there are so many card-making supplies available today.

Send your love with a cross stitch bag filled with treats. Change the fabric colour, change the design, change the treats and it becomes a gift for anyone – it might be filled with coffee beans for dad, with cosmetics for mum or with herbs or pot-pourri for a friend – the choice is endless. Display it on a door-knob or use it to scent a chest of drawers.

Sending greetings, best wishes or loving support to someone with a sachet like this would be a charming alternative to a card. Making up a sachet is simple and you can add all sorts of embellishments, such as an unusual twisted wire handle decorated with beads and ribbons.

Mini Samplers

As well as the main samplers and many smaller projects there are also designs throughout the book perfect for mini samplers – small, quick to stitch but sure to be treasured by the recipient. These designs (marked within the chart pages) are very adaptable and can be made up as simple or more complex projects. For example, add a printed fabric border and make up as a quilted hanging – minimum stitching but maximum effect! You could also stitch these designs on brightly coloured embroidery fabrics.

Personalizing Designs

There are many alphabets and numbers charted throughout the book, which will allow you to alter the lettering and dates on the main samplers and the mini samplers – in fact, any of the designs can have the addition of words or messages to make them personal to you or the recipient.

♥ Plan letters and numbers on graph paper first, to ensure they will fit the space available.

♥ If the letters or numbers won't fit, choose a smaller alphabet, or a backstitch alphabet instead of a cross stitch one. If a small motif is in the way you could move it or omit it.

♥ If a design has a border, you can enlarge the design to allow more space for wording by adding to the border length.

♥ Many projects have the addition of seed beads, small charms and other embellishments, so check out your local craft store and add some personal touches of your own.

WELCOME BABY

This chapter features delightful designs to welcome a new baby into the world, beginning with a beautiful birth sampler. For those doubly blessed, a delightful twins' sampler can be adapted for boy or girl twins. There is also a whole range of irresistible ideas for keepsake gifts, including little star hangings with cute greetings, adorable stuffed linen toys and a set of painted boxes, perfect for storing baby treasures. Why not start with some pretty tags and cards? These are so quick to make but will mean such a lot to a proud parent. As well as the stitch-off-the-page designs and other project ideas, there are additional charts that will give you plenty of inspiration for personalizing the designs and creating your own lovely projects.

Bootie Card

Stitch count: 21h x 20w
Design size: 3.8 x 3.8cm (1½ x 1½in)
This cute bootie is perfect for a baby card and very quick to stitch for a last-minute keepsake (chart on page 21). It can be stitched in any colour and here the bootie is worked alone on white 14-count Aida and mounted into a double-fold card. Add a bow of your choice – tiny bows are available in lots of colours from craft shops and scrapbook suppliers.

Birth Sampler

Stitch count: 101h x 83w
Design size: 18.3 x 15cm (7¼ x 6in)
Fabric: 28-count white linen (or 14-count Aida)
Threads: DMC stranded cotton (floss) listed in chart key
Embellishments: Tiny buttons and pins (optional)
Prepare your fabric for work. Follow the chart on page 14 and work over two linen threads (or one Aida block), using two strands of stranded cotton for full and three-quarter cross stitches and one strand for backstitches. Add the embellishments and then frame (see page 94).

Train Tag

Stitch count: 11h x 15w
Design size: 2 x 2.5cm (¾ x 1in)
Gift tags are quick to make and you are sure to be inspired by some of the gorgeous card and paper stock available. Stitch the train on page 21 on white 14-count Aida. Back the embroidery with iron-on interfacing and glue it to the tag. Use a matching ribbon as a tie.

This charming sampler for a baby boy in a simple white frame would suit any nursery and is sure to delight new parents. A delicious pink version is charted on page 15. Why not stitch a pretty gift tag too? A train is great for a little boy and a flower (see page 21) for a girl.

It's Twins!

Celebrate that most memorable of births and welcome twins into the world in colourful style with a charming birth sampler. There are also stuffed stars in pretty pastels for each of the little ones. For a quicker project, why not stitch the sweet mini samplers on page 18, so each twin has a gift all of their own?

Baby Stars

Stitch count: 55h x 47w

Design size: 10 x 8.5cm (4 x 3½in)

These sweet stars, shown below in yellow and opposite in blue and pink, can be made as individual little hangings or as a group, or even as a mobile. Stitch the motif from page 17 on white 14-count Aida using two strands of stranded cotton for cross stitches. When all stitching is complete, make up the stars as described on page 95.

Welcome Twins Sampler

Stitch count: 115h x 62w

Design size: 21 x 11.3cm (8¼ x 4½in)

Fabric: 28-count white linen (or 14-count Aida)

Threads: DMC stranded cotton (floss) listed in chart key

Prepare your fabric for work. Follow the chart on page 16 and work over two linen threads (or one Aida block), using two strands of stranded cotton for full and three-quarter cross stitches and one for backstitches. When stitching is complete, frame the sampler (see page 94).

These little tags are ideal to accompany a sampler or other gift. Stitch them as charted, or add extra rows of stitches as desired. Alternatively, use one of the other small designs charted. Make a tag by folding a piece of card in half, glue the stitching to the tag and punch a hole for a ribbon tie.

Twins are a double delight and this colourful sampler celebrates their birth beautifully. Two little stuffed stars make lovely hangings for the cot or pram and the colours are easily changed.

Baby Gifts

Gifts for babies are such fun to make and are usually small enough to be stitched in an evening or weekend. Adorable soft toys (shown right) are sure to be well loved and cuddled while little boxes (below) are perfect for preserving magical memories of a baby's early years. A hanging adorned with bells will make a baby's first Christmas a memorable one.

Baby's First Christmas

Stitch count: 29h x 29w

Design size: 5 x 5cm (2 x 2in)

Stitch this little hanging on a 12cm (5in) square of white 28-count linen using the chart on page 19, or the alternate chart there. You could also make up your own design using other motifs from this chapter. Use the alphabet and numbers on page 19 to stitch the name and date. See page 96 for making up.

Teddy Toys

Stitch counts: 27h x 21w and 34h x 48w

Design sizes: 5 x 3.8cm (2 x 1½in) and 6 x 8.8cm (2½in x 3½in)

Fabric: 28-count white or sand linen

Threads: DMC stranded cotton (floss) listed in chart key

Embellishments: Buttons and gingham ribbon

For one toy, take two 30 x 26cm (12 x 10in) pieces of linen and using washable pen, draw round the teddy shape from page 103 on one piece of linen. Turn the piece over and stitch the motif from page 18 or 21 in the centre. Work over two linen threads, using two strands for cross stitches and Algerian eyes and one for backstitches. See page 96 for making up the toy.

Craft a Keepsake . . .

♥ Make a door sign for the nursery with the Ssh... Baby's Sleeping design on page 20. Mount the stitching over stiff card and add a ribbon hanger.

♥ Stitch the welcome train from page 21 and mount into a yellow card.

♥ Adorn a newborn's photo album by stitching the duck or heart border on page 18 on Aida band.

Keepsake Boxes

Stitch count: 26h x 24w

Design size: 4.5 x 4.5cm (1¾ x 1¾in)

Little boxes like these (see Suppliers) can be decorated in many ways. Here they have been kept simple and painted white but little pots of emulsion or poster paints come in a huge range of colours.

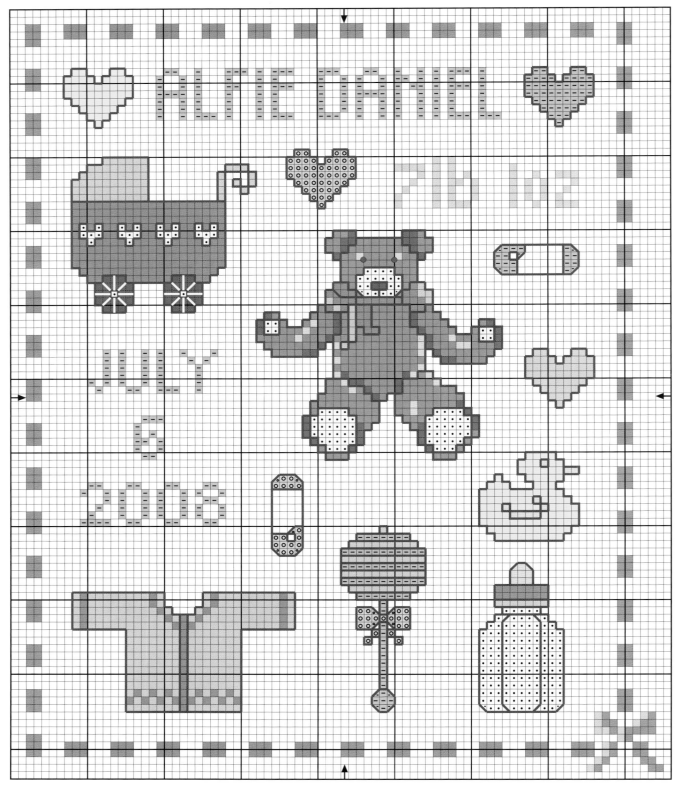

Boy Birth Sampler

DMC stranded cotton

Cross stitch (2 strands)

■ 317	▨ 437	▨ 827
− 352	□ 744	▨ 842
■ 435	▨ 799	⊙ 966

• blanc

Backstitch (1 strand)

— 317

⚊ blanc

French knots (2 strands)

● 317

Change the names and
numbers using the chart
on page 19

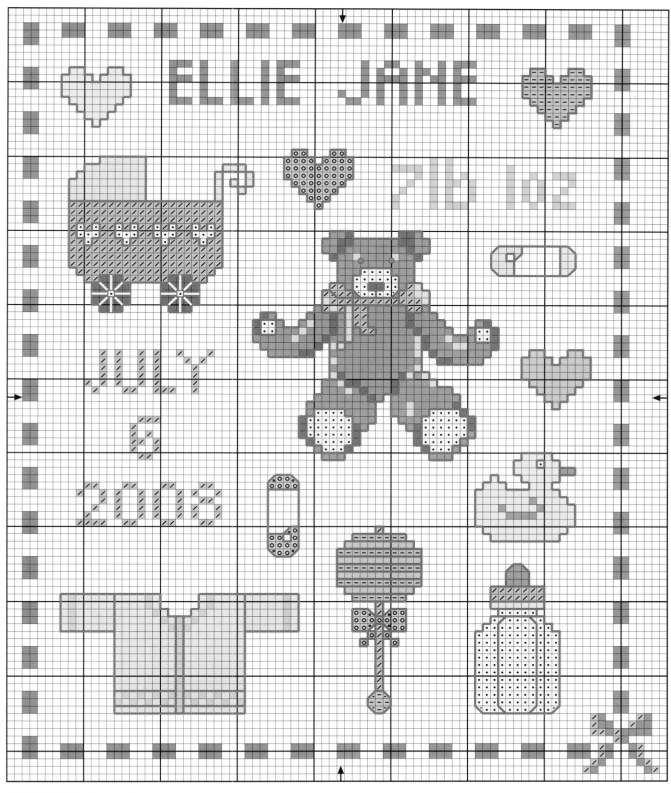

Girl Birth Sampler

DMC stranded cotton
Cross stitch (2 strands)

▢ 153	▨ 435	▢ 827	▨ 3607
− 352	▨ 437	▢ 842	╱ 3608
▨ 414	▢ 744	⊙ 966	• blanc

Backstitch (1 strand)
— 414
═ blanc

French knots (2 strands)
● 414

Change the names and
numbers using the chart
on page 19

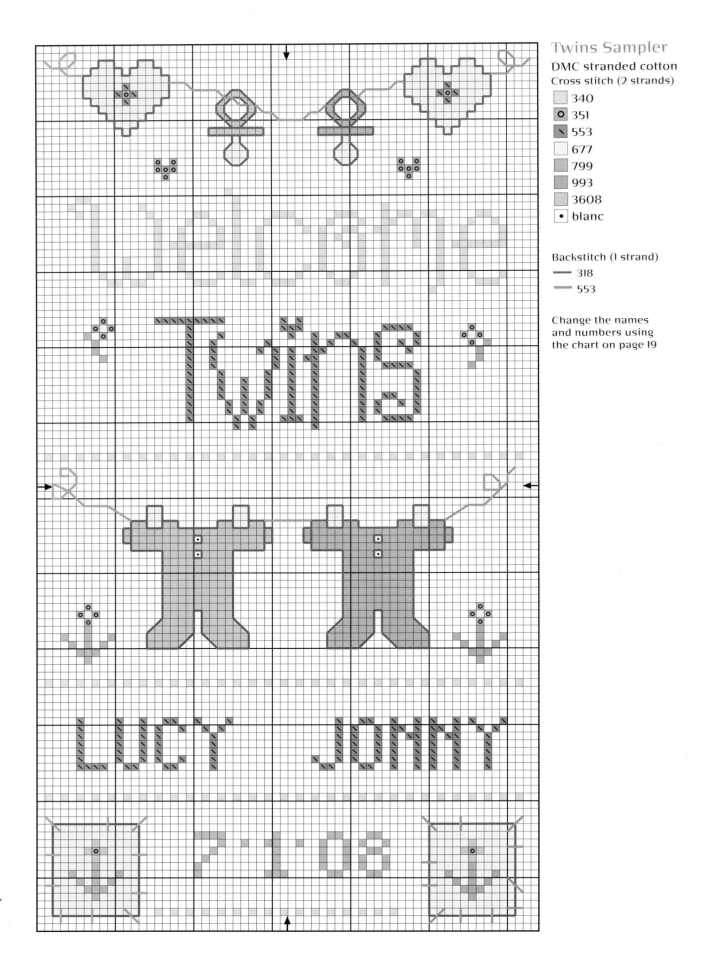

Twins Sampler

DMC stranded cotton
Cross stitch (2 strands)

- 340
- ⊙ 351
- ╲ 553
- 677
- 799
- 993
- 3608
- • blanc

Backstitch (1 strand)
— 318
— 553

Change the names and numbers using the chart on page 19

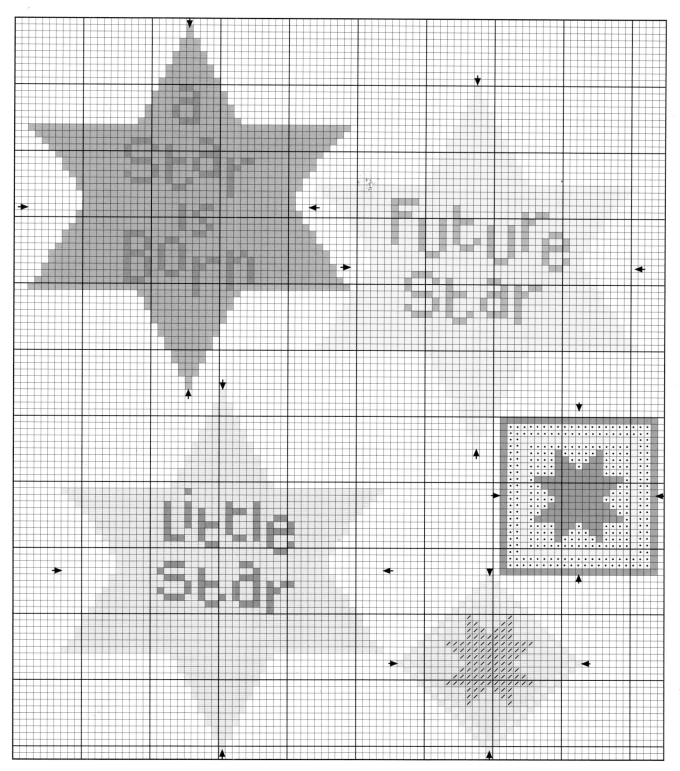

DMC stranded cotton
Cross stitch (2 strands)

✎ 340		677		• 3747	
351		794			
605		3746			

MOLLY

NEW BABY

Baby
Boy

HARRY
11·10·08

Mini samplers

The dashed red lines indicate
where to repeat the design

Baby
GIRL

MOLLY
2·1·08

DMC stranded cotton
Cross stitch (2 strands)

209	341	437	V 676	I 818	＼ ecru
317	O 352	L 472	677	3045	• blanc
— 340	／ 402	564	799	3608	

Backstitch
(1 strand)

—— 317

—— 318

French knots
(2 strands)

● 317

Change names and
numbers using the
chart opposite

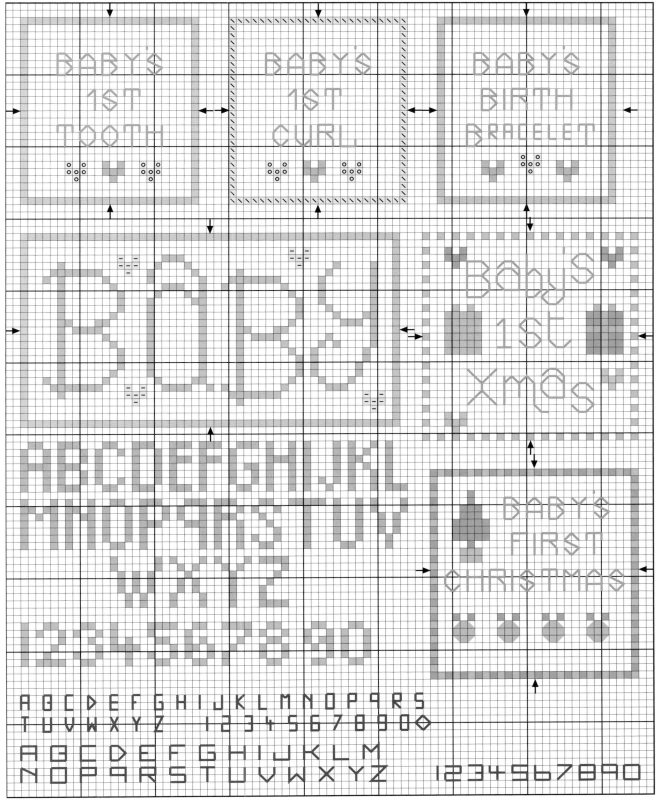

DMC stranded cotton

Cross stitch (2 strands)

▨ 352	▨ 809	◣ 3609
▨ 554	⊙ 827	
− 677	▨ 959	

Backstitch (1 strand)

— 317
— 553

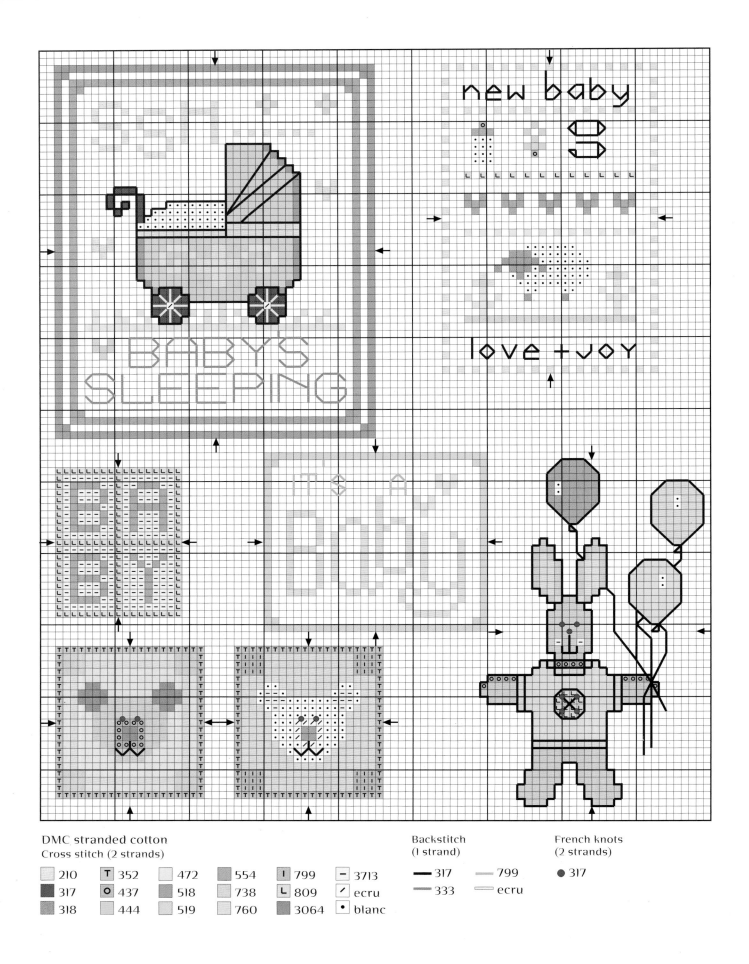

DMC stranded cotton
Cross stitch (2 strands)

▨ 210	T 352	▨ 472	▨ 554	I 799	− 3713
■ 317	O 437	▨ 518	▨ 738	L 809	⁄ ecru
▨ 318	▨ 444	▨ 519	▨ 760	▨ 3064	• blanc

Backstitch
(1 strand)

——— 317
——— 333

——— 799
═══ ecru

French knots
(2 strands)

● 317

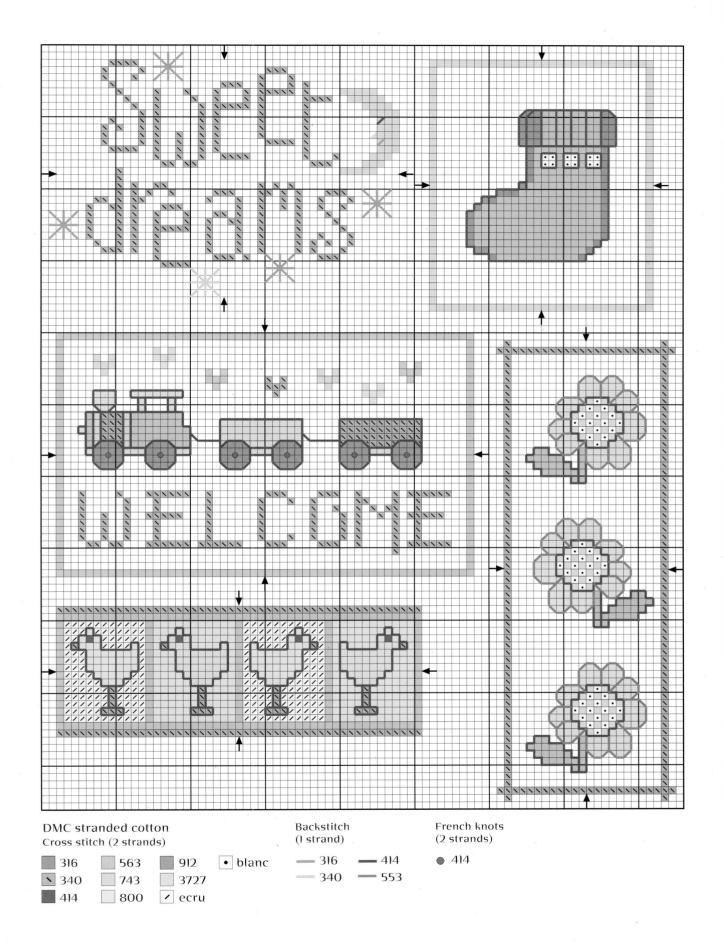

DMC stranded cotton
Cross stitch (2 strands)

316	563	912	• blanc
340	743	3727	
414	800	/ ecru	

Backstitch
(1 strand)

316 — 414
340 — 553

French knots
(2 strands)

● 414

LOVE IS IN THE AIR

This chapter is all about love and romance: the affirmation of love at a wedding and keeping love alive on occasions such as Valentine's Day. A delightful wedding sampler complete with a sugar-pink cake sparkling with beads looks lovely mounted in a simple white frame. The design has a matching ring pillow and place card. For a wonderfully romantic Valentine's Day there is a lovely stitched and beaded heart in its own painted box. There are plenty of romantic designs charted in this chapter, with lots of ideas on how to use them. Stitch some of the mini sampler designs or use the gorgeous hearts on page 29 to send love and good wishes. There are tiny hearts too that could be stitched as patches for cards and tags.

Wedding Card

Stitch count: *35h x 32w*
Design size: *6.3 x 5.8cm*
(2½ x 2¼in)

A lovely wedding card is quick to make, especially if you use a ready-made card mount. Embellish the card with wedding-theme charms, buttons and celebration stick-ons.

Wedding Sampler

Stitch count: 106h x 86w
Design size: 19.2 x 15.6cm (7½ x 6⅛in)
Fabric: 28-count antique white linen (or 14-count Aida)
Threads: DMC stranded cotton listed in chart key
Embellishments: Mill Hill pink seed beads and tiny white heart buttons

Prepare your fabric for work. Follow the chart on page 26 and work over two linen threads (or one Aida block), using two strands of stranded cotton for cross stitch and one for backstitch. Change names and dates using the chart on page 32, planning them out on graph paper to ensure they fit the space. Sew on the buttons and beads. See page 94 for framing.

Place Name Card

Stitch count: 14h x 15w
(motif only)
Design size: 2.5 x 2.5cm
(1 x 1in)

With just a small cross stitch motif and some ribbon you can create some stylish place cards for weddings and other celebratory occasions. Stitch a rose from page 26 on 14-count Aida. Back the stitching with iron-on interfacing and cut out around the rose. Glue the stitching to a folded card, over a strip of cream ribbon.

A contemporary wedding sampler, mounted in a simple white frame, records the event in charming style.

Given with Love

This section shows how easy it is to create a range of lovely gifts to give to those you love and admire, whether it's to celebrate the special event of an engagement or wedding, or because it's Valentine's Day and you want to send loving thoughts.

Wedding Ring Pillow

Stitch count: 64h x 84w
Design size: 11.6 x 15.2cm (4½ x 6in)
Fabric: 28-count white linen
Threads: DMC stranded cotton listed in chart key
Embellishments: Pink sequins and cream ribbon

A ring pillow makes a charming memento of a special day. Fill it with scented pot-pourri for a nice finishing touch. Follow the chart on page 27 and work over two linen threads. When stitching is complete, attach narrow cream ribbon and sew pink sequins around the initials. Make up following step 1 for Baby's First Christmas on page 96.

Craft a Keepsake...

♥ Stitch the Follow Your Heart chart or With Love chart on page 29 and make up as an ornament in a similar way to the Valentine Heart opposite.

♥ The patchwork hearts on page 29 are perfect for gift tags. Stitch them on perforated paper, glue card on the back and cut out to make tags, adding a ribbon loop.

♥ Stitch Love Makes the World Go Round on page 31 and insert into a box with a circular lid aperture. Paint the box to match the design.

♥ The little posy design on page 30 would be lovely stitched and made up into a drawstring bag as a gift for a bridesmaid.

A ring pillow is a charming way to ensure wedding rings are kept safe. The style matches the Wedding Sampler and the two would make a memorable gift.

This delicious beaded Valentine Heart presented in its own box makes a real gift to treasure. The box, with a circular lid aperture, has been painted to tone with the embroidery and a saying stitched on beige 14-count Aida inserted in the lid.

Valentine Heart

Stitch count: 56h x 49w

Design size: 10.2 x 9cm (4 x 3½in)

This gorgeous design will send love in the most romantic style. You could change the message using the alphabet on page 32 – see page 7 for personalizing designs. Follow the chart on page 28 and work over one block of white 14-count Aida, using two strands for cross stitch. When stitching is complete, sew on the beads and see page 96 for making up the heart.

Sweetheart Box

Stitch count: 41h x 41w

Design size: 7.5 x 7.5cm (3 x 3in)

Many stores now stock these versatile aperture boxes. This one has been painted with cream craft paint but it could be decorated with embellishments too, such as stick-on hearts and flowers. Follow the chart on page 28 and work over one block of 14-count beige Aida. When stitching is complete, insert the embroidery into a box with a 9.5cm (3¾in) aperture lid, trimming the stitching if necessary.

Stitch the heart
motif if not using a
heart button

Wedding Sampler

DMC stranded cotton

Cross stitch (2 strands)

▨	151	▨ 415	◉ 722	• blanc	
▨	316	▨ 422	◥ 778		
▨	340	▨ 704	▬ 3042		

Backstitch (1 strand)

— 315
— 414
— 704

Mill Hill seed beads

◉ 72053 pink

Change the names, initials
and dates using the chart
on page 32

DMC stranded cotton

Cross stitch (2 strands)

▨ 316	⊙ 772	• blanc	
▨ 340	↘ 778		
▨ 704	– 3042		

Backstitch (1 strand)

— 315
— 704

Change the initials using
the chart on page 33

DMC stranded cotton
Cross stitch (2 strands)

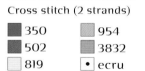 350   954

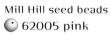 502   3832

819   • ecru

Mill Hill seed beads
62005 pink

DMC stranded cotton
Cross stitch (2 strands)

340	503	3608	• ecru	
341	718	3609		
502	726	3746		

Backstitch (1 strand)
— 3746

Change the initials using
the chart on page 32

Mini sampler

Ring position

With this ring

YOU HOLD THE KEY TO MY HEART

THINGS ARE BETTER WITH TWO

YOU'LL ALWAYS HAVE MY HEART

DMC stranded cotton
Cross stitch (2 strands)

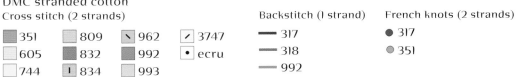

351	809	962	3747
605	832	992	ecru
744	834	993	

Backstitch (1 strand)
— 317
— 318
— 992

French knots (2 strands)
● 317
● 351

DMC stranded cotton
Cross stitch (2 strands)

▨ 341	✓ 604	▨ 799	▨ 3053	• ecru	
V 522	▨ 743	I 834	o 3806		
▨ 603	▨ 744	– 842	▨ 3832		

Backstitch
(1 strand)

— 317
— 522

French knots
(2 strands)

● 317

Mill Hill seed beads

◉ 00557 gold
◉ 62035 pink

DMC stranded cotton
Cross stitch (2 strands)

✔ 350	602	I 743	− 842	＼ 3053	
V 543	O 604	744	958		
553	605	809	3052		

Backstitch
(1 strand)

— 317 — 958
— 602 — 3746

French knots
(2 strands)

● 602

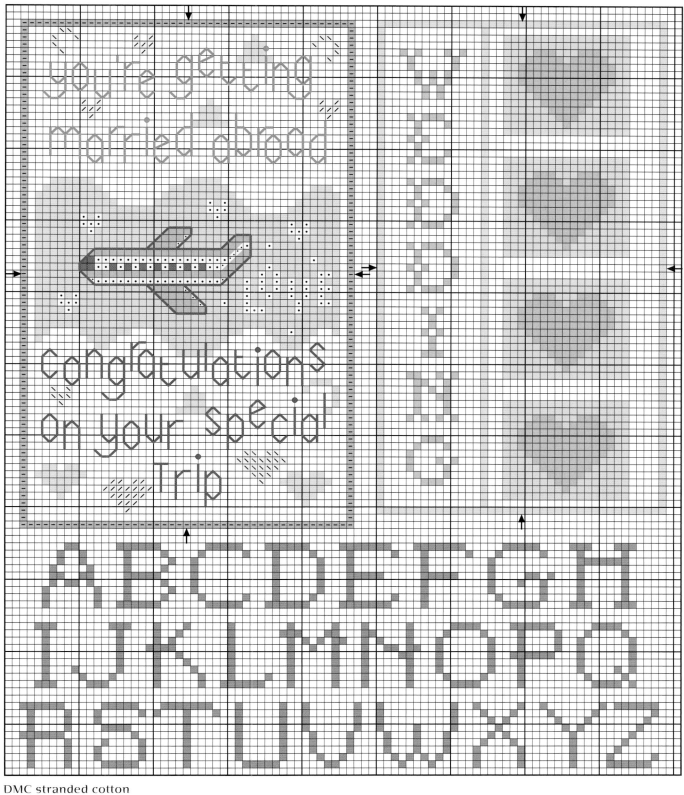

You're getting
married abroad

Congratulations
on your special
Trip

ABCDEFGH
IJKLMNOPQ
RSTUVWXYZ

DMC stranded cotton
Cross stitch (2 strands)

					Backstitch (1 strand)	French knots (2 strand)
↘ 151		414		827	— 414	● 414
316	✓	745		899	— 3838	● 3838
– 340		772	•	blanc		

ANNIVERSARY CELEBRATIONS

Stitched gifts and keepsakes are always very welcome ways to celebrate an anniversary and provide a lasting reminder of the event, and there are lots of lovely ideas in this chapter. For a quick project make stylish hanging anniversary sachets, one for 25, 40, and 50 year anniversaries. You'll find plenty of smaller designs suitable for cards and gift tags, so you could soon stitch a small personalized design to add to any gift. Gifts and keepsakes to recall those anniversary memories include a beautiful, romantic anniversary sampler mounted into a white wooden box and a pretty bottle label, suitable to celebrate any kind of anniversary. The designs charted on page 42 could also be stitched as mini samplers, personalizing them with the alphabets provided.

Anniversary Sachet Hangings

Stitch count: 70h x 67w
Design size: 12.7 x 12cm (5 x 4¾in)
Fabric: 28-count white, pale pink or sand linen
Threads: DMC stranded cotton listed in chart key
Embellishments: Mother-of-pearl buttons

The charming hanging sachets shown here make the perfect gift to celebrate any anniversary – simply change the number using the chart on page 43. Decorate the sachets with mother-of-pearl buttons and fill them with scented pot-pourri. Follow the charts on page 39–41 and work over two threads of linen using two strands for cross stitch and one strand for backstitches and Algerian eyes. When stitching is complete, sew on the buttons and make up following steps 1 and 2 for the Affirmation Wishes pillow on page 100, adding a ribbon loop for hanging before over sewing the gap.

Craft a Keepsake...

♥ Why not make some gift cards for special anniversaries when you have a spare moment, so that you will always have a selection ready?

♥ You could add charms to the Anniversary Sachets that relate to the particular year being celebrated, for example a gold ring, a silver thimble, ruby crystal heart and so on.

♥ Stitch the Happy Times chart on page 42 and mount it on a photo album or scrapbook for anniversary memories.

Anniversary Memories

It's easy and enjoyable to create gifts and mementoes of an anniversary or a special occasion to be remembered. A sampler box is perfect for holding treasured reminders, such as love letters, locks of hair, photos and other small keepsakes. An embellished bottle of champagne is sure to be appreciated to celebrate any event.

Bottle Label

Stitch count: 49h x 30w
Design size: 9 x 5.4cm (3½ x 2⅛in)

Turn a celebratory bottle of wine or bubbly into something really special with this romantic label. Add a little tag and you have the perfect gift to start a celebration off in style. You could also use the Happy Times design charted on page 42. See page 97 for the fabric needed. Follow the chart on page 42 and work over two threads of cream 28-count linen (or 14-count Aida). When all the stitching is completed see page 97 for making up the label.

Anniversary Box Sampler

Stitch count: 60h x 84w
Design size: 11 x 15.2cm (4¼ x 6in)
Fabric: 28-count antique white linen
Threads: DMC stranded cotton listed in chart key
Embellishments: Mill Hill red seed beads and a mother-of-pearl button

Prepare your fabric for work. Follow the chart overleaf and work over two linen threads (or one block of 14-count Aida), using two strands of stranded cotton for cross stitch and one for backstitch and the star-like Algerian eye stitches. Change the initials and dates using the chart on page 43. When all stitching is complete sew on the beads with a beading needle and then sew on the button. Insert the stitching into the box lid or frame it as a sampler.

Craft a Keepsake...

♥ Stitch the rose border from page 43 on a strip of Aida band to make a ribbon to tie around a gift of a plant, and make a tag to match using the pink heart motif.

♥ Change the colours of the flower charted on page 41 to match those of a special bouquet and mount into a card and decorate the card with celebration-themed embellishments.

♥ Stitch the row of tulips charted on page 38 on linen or Aida band and repeat the design as often as necessary to decorate bath towels or bed linen.

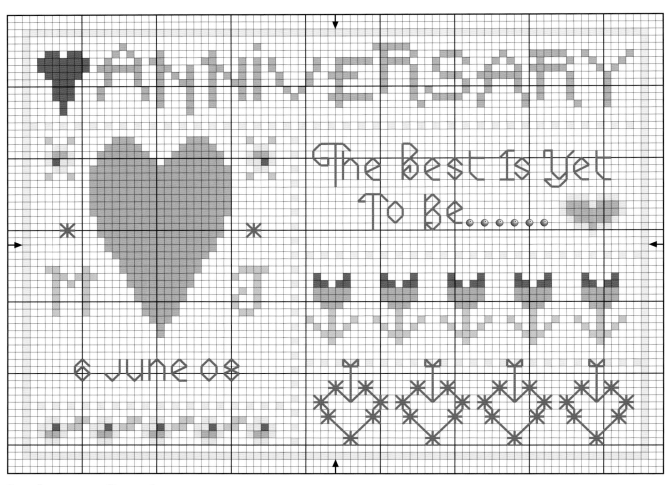

Anniversary Sampler

DMC stranded cotton

Cross stitch (2 strands)	Backstitch (1 strand)	Algerian eyes (1 strand)	Mill Hill seed beads	Change the initials and date using the chart on page 43.

Cross stitch (2 strands)	Backstitch (1 strand)	Algerian eyes (1 strand)	Mill Hill seed beads
316	— 3726	✳ 3726	● 62012 dark red
503			
778			
3726			

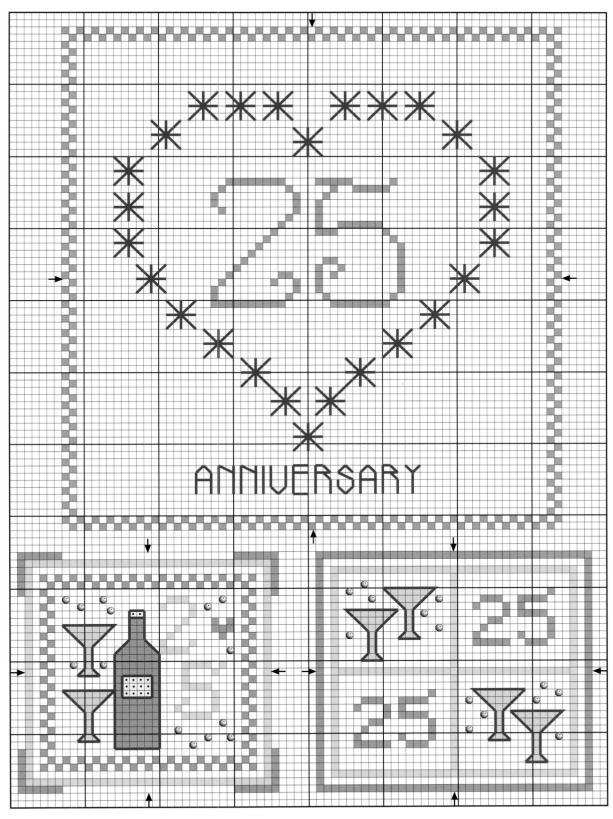

DMC stranded cotton

Cross stitch (2 strands)	Backstitch (1 strand)	Algerian eyes (1 strand)	Mill Hill seed beads	Change the large number using the chart on page 43

519

—930

✳ 930

● 02064 blue

932

• ecru

ANNIVERSARY

Happy Anniversary

Anniversary Greetings

DMC stranded cotton

Cross stitch
(2 strands)

■ 315	▨ 3042
▨ 316	▨ 3840
▨ 503	

Backstitch
(1 strand)

— 315
— 503

Algerian eyes
(1 strand)

✳ 315

French knots
(2 strands)

● 315

Change the large
number using the
chart on page 43

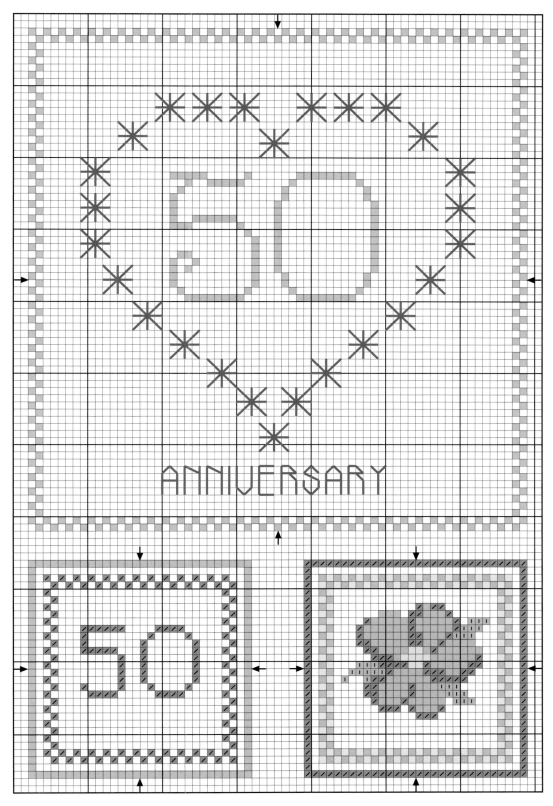

DMC stranded cotton

Cross stitch (2 strands)		Backstitch (1 strand)	Algerian eyes (1 strand)	Change the large number using the chart on page 43
▨ 223	☐ 519	— 350	✳ 350	
▨ 352	▮ 3766			

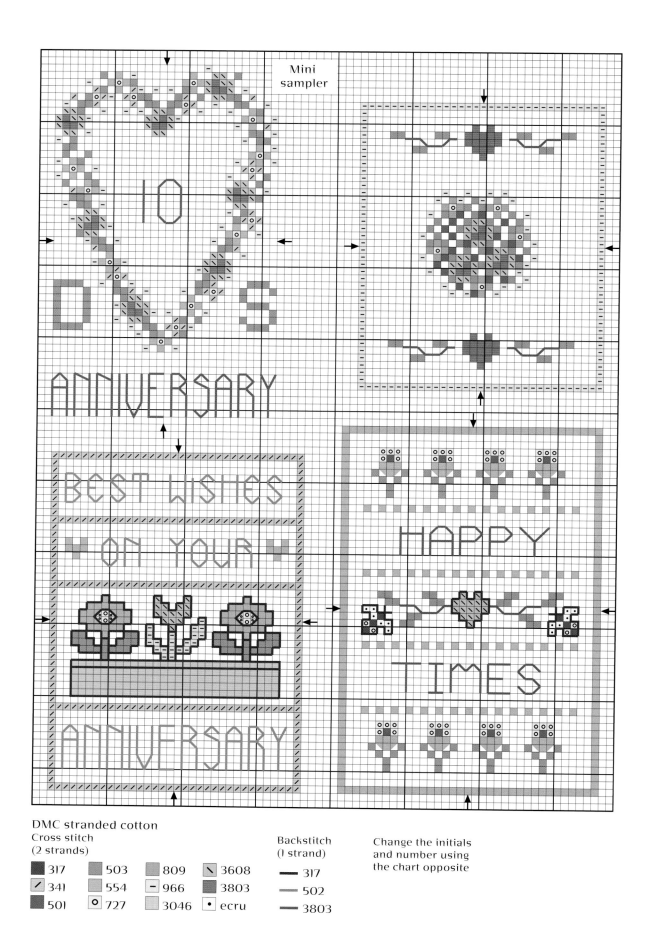

Mini sampler

DMC stranded cotton
Cross stitch
(2 strands)

■ 317	■ 503	■ 809	＼ 3608
／ 341	■ 554	－ 966	■ 3803
■ 501	○ 727	■ 3046	• ecru

Backstitch
(1 strand)

— 317

— 502

— 3803

Change the initials
and number using
the chart opposite

DMC stranded cotton

Cross stitch
(2 strands)

▨ 223   • 818

▨ 503   ◹ 899

Backstitch
(1 strand)

— 317

Use the alphabets and
numbers here to personalize
your stitching, changing the
colours as desired

SCHOOL DAYS

This chapter focuses on school children, teachers and education. First, there are those memorable early days at school, followed by acknowledging the part a dedicated teacher can play in our lives, and on to the students – all stars in their own way. A charming quilted hanger (shown right) is a lovely keepsake for that exciting first day at school. A bright and fresh children's alphabet can be used on many projects and to personalize a whole range of children's gifts. Two examples are shown here – a delightful bag, which is sure to thrill any little girl, and a cheeky monkey on a little boy's pencil case. There are also many smaller designs and mini samplers, with suggestions overleaf and on page 48 for how to use them.

Alphabet Bag

Stitch count: 15h x 22w for motif shown
Design size: 2.5 x 4cm (1 x 1½in)
This gorgeous little bag is made from blue and white ticking and decorated with pretty flower buttons and a stitched patch with the child's initial. For the perfect gift, fill the bag with treats. Stitch one of the letters from the chart on pages 50–51 on 14-count white Aida. See page 98 for making up the bag.

First Day Quilted Hanging

Stitch count: 71h x 51w
Design size: 12.7 x 9.5cm (5 x 3¾in)
Fabric: 28-count white linen (or 14-count Aida)
Threads: DMC stranded cotton listed in chart key
Embellishments: Two mother-of-pearl buttons, string handle
Prepare your fabric for work and mark the centre point. Follow the chart on page 52 and work over two linen threads (or one Aida block) using two strands of stranded cotton for full and three-quarter cross stitches and one strand for backstitches. When stitching is completed see page 97 for making up the hanging.

Monkey Pencil Case

Stitch count: 15h x 27w
Design size: 2.5 x 5cm (1 x 2in)
This useful project is a quick-stitch gift for a child starting school. For an extra surprise add some crayons to the case. Stitch one of the letters from pages 50–51 on 14-count white Aida. Iron fusible webbing on the back of the stitching. Trim to size and glue to the pencil case or other item of your choice, such as a ruler or bookmark.

A mini sampler makes a cheerful hanger when teamed with red and white gingham. A children's alphabet provides lots of bright ideas for projects, such as a cheeky monkey pencil case.

Best Teacher

Caring and dedicated teachers remain long in our memories and the projects on these pages acknowledge their importance. For that special teacher stitch a delightfully warm sampler that affirms their importance in young lives. A stuffed apple with a Best Teacher label is easy to create and fun to do. See below for other ideas on using the designs charted in this chapter.

Craft a Keepsake. . .

♥ Create a really special thank you card for a favourite teacher by stitching Best Teacher (charted on page 53) on to 14-count Aida. Cut out the stitching, mount it on a card and add embellishments and ribbons.

♥ Make a special gift tag for a teacher's end-of-term gift by stitching You're the Best (page 55) on to 14-count Aida. Cut out and glue to a small card, then punch a hole in the top right corner and add a matching ribbon.

♥ Paint a papier mâche aperture-lid box in a bright colour. Stitch a teacher's initials from the alphabet chart (pages 50–51) on 14-count white Aida, cut out and insert in the box lid.

To Teach Sampler

Stitch count: 118h x 48w
Design size: 23 x 9.5cm (9 x 3¾in)
Fabric: 25-count driftwood Dublin linen
Threads: DMC stranded cotton listed in chart key

Prepare your fabric for work and mark the centre. Follow the chart on page 54 and work over two threads of linen, using two strands of stranded cotton for full and three-quarter cross stitches and one strand for backstitches. Use two strands for the variegated thread. If desired, you could use a Color Variations thread 4200 for the border instead of DMC 223. When stitching is complete, frame your sampler – see page 94.

Apple for Teacher

Stitch count: 15h x 27w
Design size: 2.5 x 5cm (1 x 2in)

This project is great fun. You could stitch the apple with bright green threads instead of red if you prefer. Stitch the motifs from page 53 and 55 over one block of white 14-count Aida. When the stitching is complete, fray the edges of the Best Teacher label and see page 99 for making up the apple.

The To Teach sampler is a warm affirmation of the great importance teachers have in children's lives. The stuffed apple is a fun idea and quick to make – why not stitch several for your child's favourite teachers?

Best Student

Celebrate a child's achievements at school with a range of gifts and keepsakes. Start with a special cover for a photo album to capture the many milestone pictures of a child's first year at school. As children grow older and exams become a focal point in their educational life, why not make them their very own Study Buddy, with an affirming and encouraging message attached to help keep them thinking positively.

Study Buddies

Stitch count: 29h x 29w and 18h x 29w for motifs shown

Design size: 5 x 5cm (2 x 2in) and 3.2 x 5cm (1¼ x 2in)

The adorable little study buddies shown below are simple to make and you can add any of the affirmations from the chart pages or create your own. Stitch the affirmation on to 14-count Aida and then see page 99 for making up the buddies.

First Year Album

Stitch count: 98h x 71w

Design size: 17.8 x 12.7cm (7 x 5in)

Fabric: 28-count pale blue linen

Threads: DMC stranded cotton listed in chart key

Embellishments: Red gingham ribbon

The album is covered in three parts – front, spine and back – so stitch the design on a piece of linen big enough to cover the front of the album, with enough for turnings. Follow the chart on page 52 and work over two linen threads using two strands of stranded cotton for full and three-quarter cross stitches. Use one strand for grey and black backstitch and two strands for white backstitch. Change the lettering and dates as required. When all the stitching is complete, see page 98 for making up the album cover.

Craft a Keepsake...

♥ Make a keepsake gift for a hardworking pupil by stitching the child's initial from the alphabet overleaf, plus one of the toys, on a patch of 14-count white Aida and use fusible web to attach it to a drawstring bag.

♥ Create a special exam success card by stitching Believe in Yourself from page 55 on to perforated paper. Cut it out, glue it on to bright card, and attach to a greetings card. Add good luck embellishments to the card.

♥ Work the Be Lucky chart from page 55 in shiny seed beads, cut it out and glue it to a pencil pot. Glue on gold or silver braid to frame the design.

♥ Make a door sign for a child's room using the chart on page 57, changing the name using the alphabet provided. Glue the stitching to stiff card and add a ribbon loop for a hanger.

A cheerful album cover celebrates a first year at school in colourful style – perfect for photographs and those endearing early drawings and paintings.

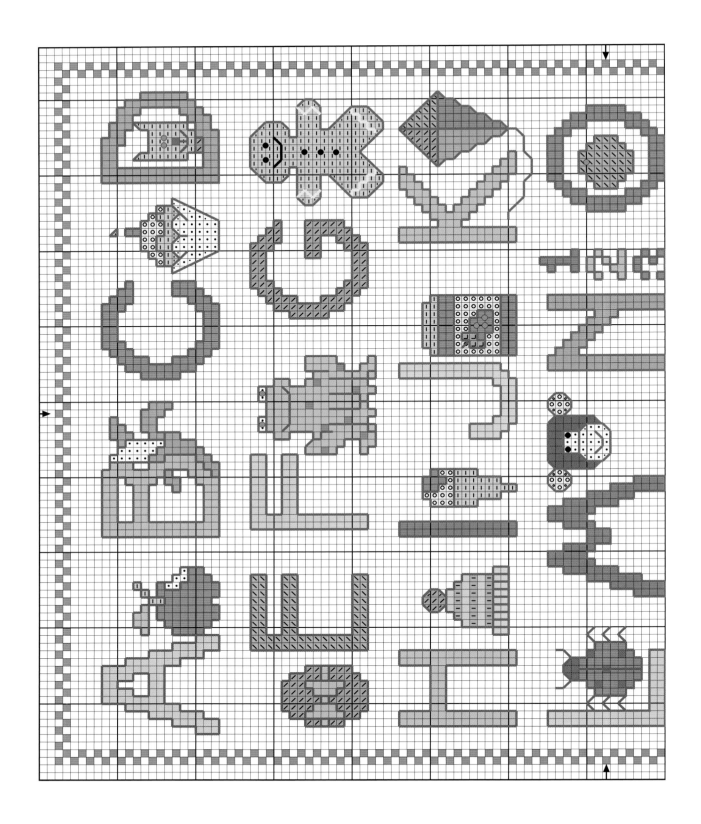

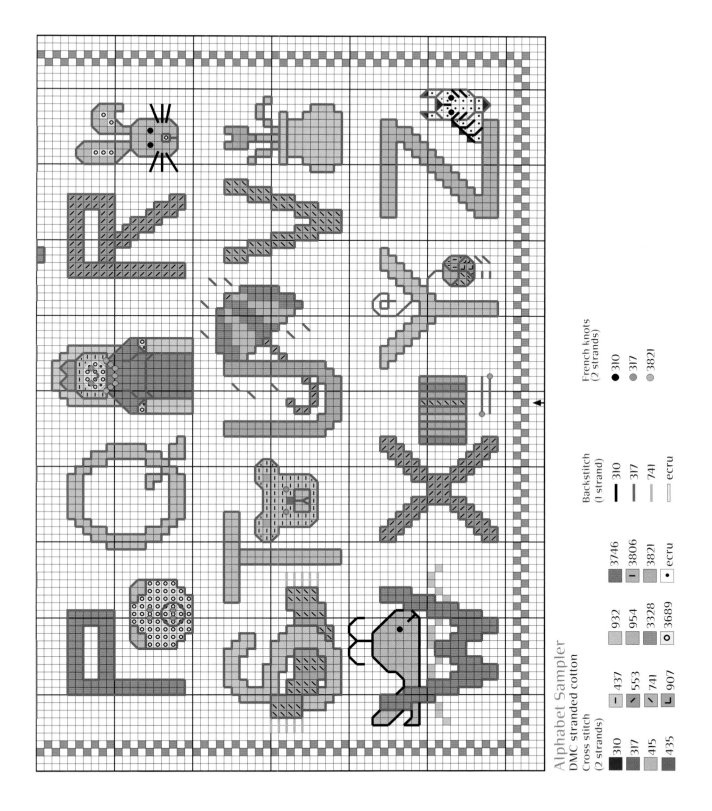

Alphabet Sampler
DMC stranded cotton

Cross stitch
(2 strands)

▉	310		932		3746	
▉	317	– 437	954	I 3806	
▉	415	✕ 553	3328	3821	
	435	✗ 741	3689	• ecru	
		L 907	○ 3821		

Backstitch
(1 strand)

▬▬	310
▬▬	317
▬▬	741
▭▭	ecru

French knots
(2 strands)

●	310
●	317
●	3821

51

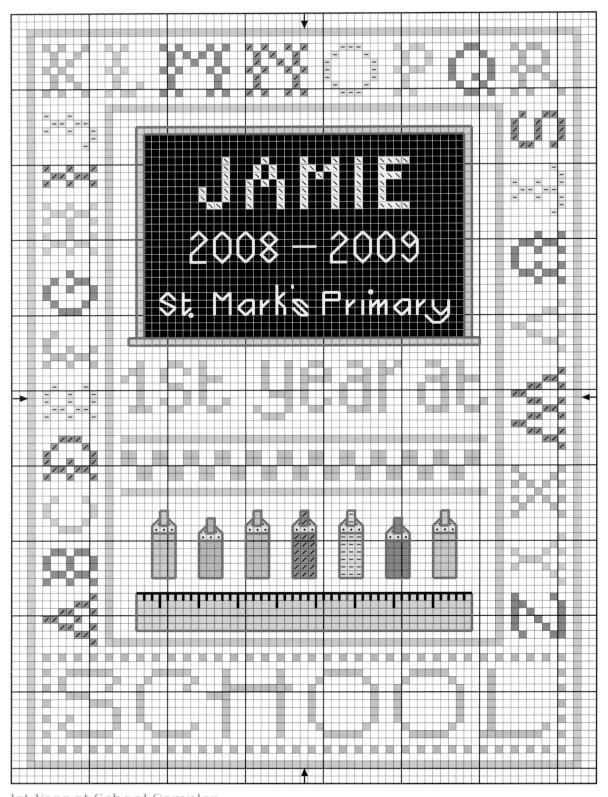

1st Year at School Sampler
DMC stranded cotton

Cross stitch (2 strands)

223	437	• 842	◣ blanc
■ 310	704	3746	
◢ 351	809	– 3766	

Backstitch

— 310 (1 strand)

— 317 (1 strand)

═ blanc (2 strands)

French knots (2 strands)

○ blanc

Change the
lettering,
numbers and
dates using the
charts on pages
19 and 54

Mini sampler

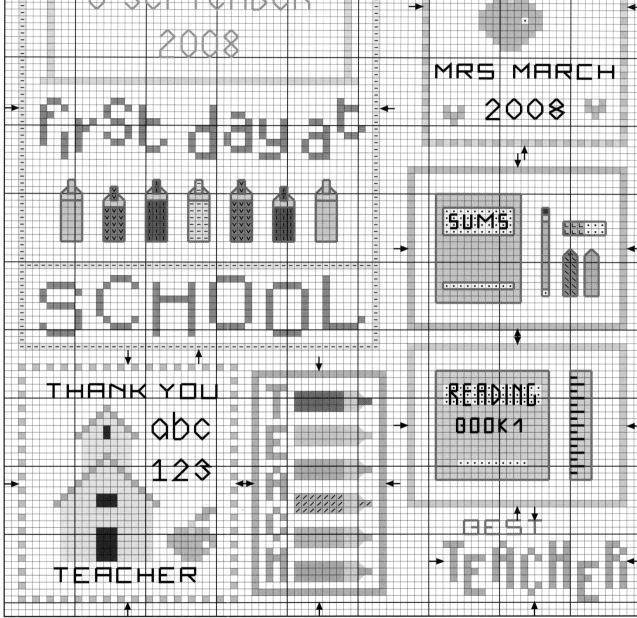

DMC stranded cotton
Cross stitch (2 strands)

	223		317		778		3053	✔	3838	•	ecru
	310	ᴸ	318		809		3832		3839		
↘	316		437	–	827	⊥	3835	↗	3854		

Backstitch (1 strand)
— 310
— 317
— 3838

Change the lettering, numbers and dates using the charts on pages 19 and 32

To Teach Sampler

DMC stranded cotton
Cross stitch (2 strands)

▨	223
▨	340
▨	347
▨	807
▨	824
▨	839
▨	3052
⧅	3827
•	ecru
V	Color Variations 4210

Backstitch (1 strand)
—— 839

Use these letters and numbers to personalize your samplers, using DMC 317 for the backstitch or other colour of your choice

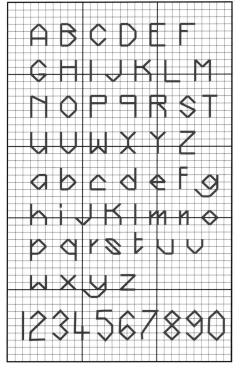

54

DMC stranded cotton
Cross stitch (2 strands)

209	✎ 340	3047	▮ 3838
223	349	3746	• blanc
317	827	3835	

Backstitch (1 strand)
— 223
— 317
— 349
— 3838

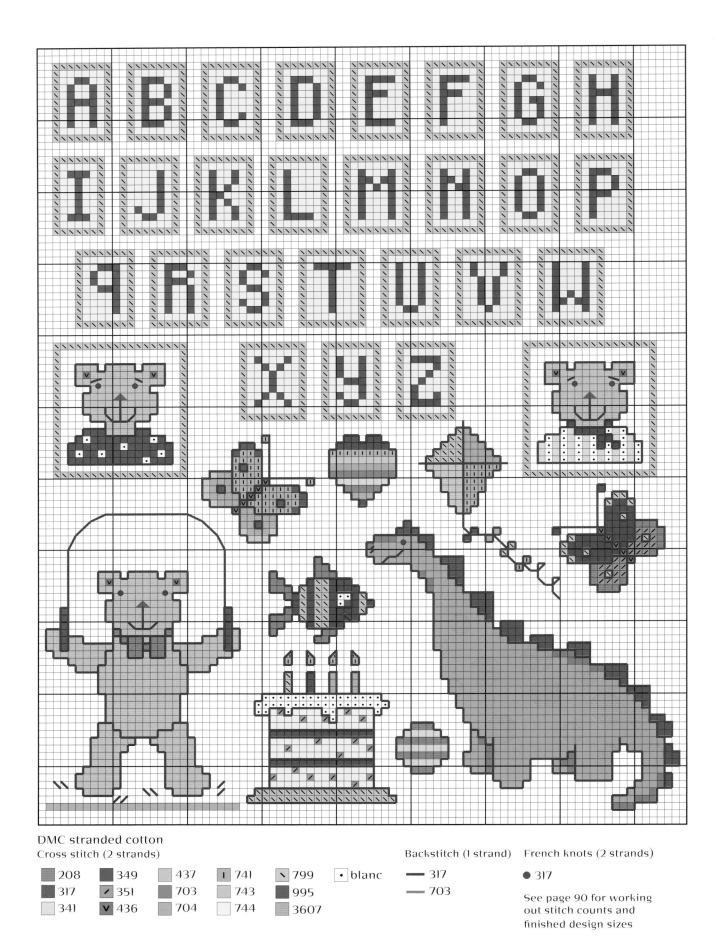

DMC stranded cotton
Cross stitch (2 strands)

								Backstitch (1 strand)	French knots (2 strands)
208	349	437	741	799	blanc		317	317
317	351	703	743	995			703	
341	436	704	744	3607				See page 90 for working out stitch counts and finished design sizes

DMC stranded cotton

Cross stitch (2 strands)

⟍ 340	744	996	⟋ 3815
350	− 842	3608	3816
▮ 718	995	3746	• ecru

Backstitch (1 strand)

— 317

French knots (2 strands)

● 317

PASTURES NEW

This chapter is devoted to change of all kinds – from moving house to changing job and on through to retirement. It's so easy to create mementoes of life-changing events and send your warmest good wishes with the designs charted here. There are designs for new jobs, travelling to pastures new, moving abroad and for finally stepping off the treadmill. A charming new home sampler, complete with idyllic cottage, celebrates the joy of a new home. Encourage someone starting a new job or being promoted with a customized pencil pot, complete with good luck tag. There are many designs to use for cards, such as the retirement card overleaf.

Spoon Ribbon Band

Stitch count: 10h x length as desired
Design size: 2cm (¾in) x length as desired
The giving of a wooden spoon is a long-standing tradition, usually to a bride on her wedding day but this charming bundle tied with a hand-stitched band would also make a lovely house-warming gift. Follow the chart on page 66, work the design on 2.5cm (1in) wide white 14-count Aida band, working from the centre outwards and repeating the pattern as desired. Hem the ends of the Aida band to finish.

New Home Sampler

Stitch count: 80h x 75w
Design size: 14.5 x 13.5cm (5¾ x 5½in)
Fabric: 28-count antique white linen
Threads: DMC stranded cotton (floss) listed in chart key

Prepare your fabric for work and mark the centre. Use the chart on page 62 and work over two linen threads using two strands of stranded cotton for full and three-quarter cross stitches and one for backstitch. When stitching is complete, frame your sampler.

New Job Pen Pot

Stitch count: 25h x 26w (excluding border)
Design size: 4.5 x 4.7cm (1¾ x 1¾in)

A handmade keepsake for someone changing jobs or receiving a promotion is sure to be much appreciated. Follow the chart on page 65 and work over two threads of 28-count cream linen. See page 100 for making up. You could also stitch a good luck tag – see chart on page 67 and making up on page 100.

A delightful New Home sampler celebrates moving into a dream home, while a pretty ribbon tying some wooden spoons together makes a charming gift.

Good Wishes

The projects shown here are all great ways to send good wishes to someone in your life about to embark on a new adventure. The hanging ornament shown opposite makes a great souvenir. Instead of a retirement card why not stitch the delightful mini sampler on page 66 to record the event? See the chart pages for other cheerful good wishes.

Moving Abroad Hanger

Stitch count: 67h x 65w
Design size: 12 x 11.5cm (4¾ x 4½in)

This hanging ornament is a bright, lively design and fun to decorate with beads, ribbons and embellishments. Follow the chart on page 67 and work over two threads of white 28-count linen. When stitching is complete, sew on two tiny heart buttons and a tiny seagull button and make up as for Affirmation Wishes on page 100. Add a Bon Voyage tag using the chart on page 67 (see page 100 for making up).

Retirement Card

Stitch count: 24h x 31w
Design size: 4.3 x 5.6cm (1¾ x 2¼in)

This bright and zingy retirement card is perfect to send good wishes to someone moving on to a new way of life. Following the chart on page 66 but stitching only the inner part of the design, work over one block of white 14-count Aida. When stitching is complete mount into a cream card. Add embellishments of your choice and create a message using rubber-stamped or stick-on letters.

Luggage Label

Stitch count: 20h x 43w
Design size: 3.8 x 7.5cm (1½ x 3in)

The good will message stitched for this fun luggage label could be worked in another colour to match the label you have chosen. Follow the chart on page 67, working over two threads of white 28-count linen. When stitching is complete, mount into your luggage label.

Craft a Keepsake...

♥ The mini retirement sampler on page 66 would make a delightful little picture or a cover for a gift of a gardening journal.

♥ Make a pretty bookmark by stitching the tall purple flower in a pot from the New Home sampler chart overleaf on to cream perforated paper. Cut out the design and glue it to a piece of card.

♥ Stitch Happy New Home from page 63 and insert it into a key ring.

♥ For someone emigrating, stitch Be Happy in Your New Life from page 64 and mount on to a photo album for keepsake photos of their new country.

The Moving Abroad Hanger makes a wonderful souvenir to take away to pastures new. Team it with a Bon Voyage Tag or change the message to one of your own.

New Home Sampler
DMC stranded cotton
Cross stitch (2 strands)

■ 310	L 340	■ 552	□ 800	■ 3347	○ 3608	
■ 317	✗ 435	■ 554	╲ 809	■ 3348	V 3822	
■ 318	I 437	− 677	■ 3045	■ 3607	• ecru	

Backstitch (1 strand)

— 317
— 552
— 3347
═ ecru

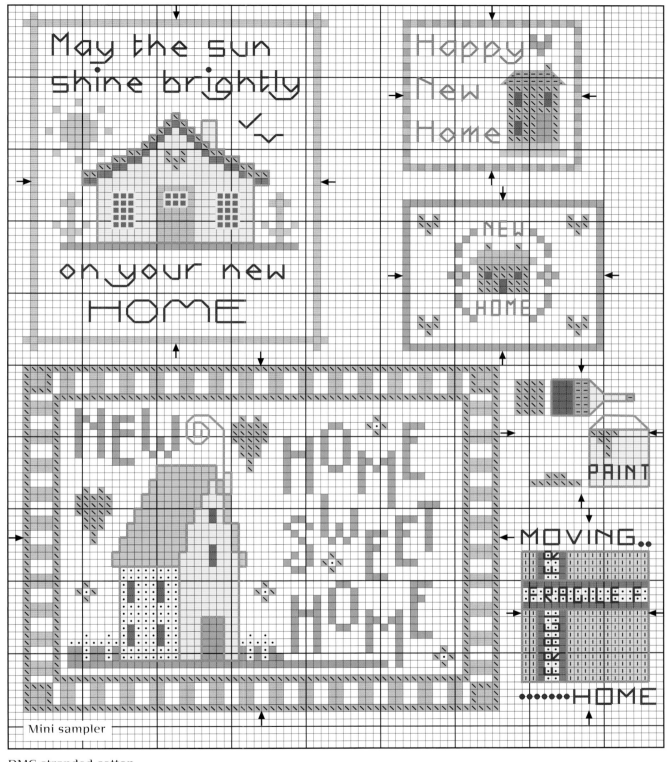

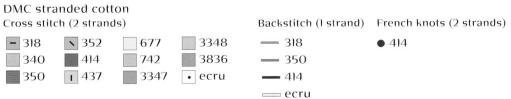

Mini sampler

DMC stranded cotton
Cross stitch (2 strands)

- 318	﹨ 352	677	3348
340	414	742	3836
350	I 437	3347	• ecru

Backstitch (1 strand)
— 318
— 350
— 414
═ ecru

French knots (2 strands)
● 414

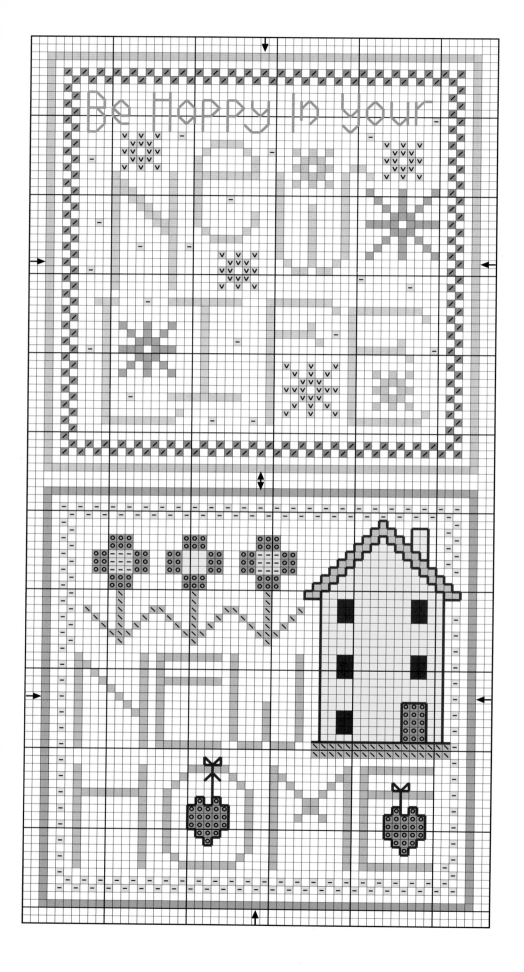

DMC stranded cotton
Cross stitch (2 strands)

- 209
- 317
- 340
- ` \ ` 368
- 677
- ` - ` 743
- 959
- 3328
- ` o ` 3608
- ` / ` 3746
- ` V ` Color Variations 4110

Backstitch (1 strand)
- —— 317
- —— 3746

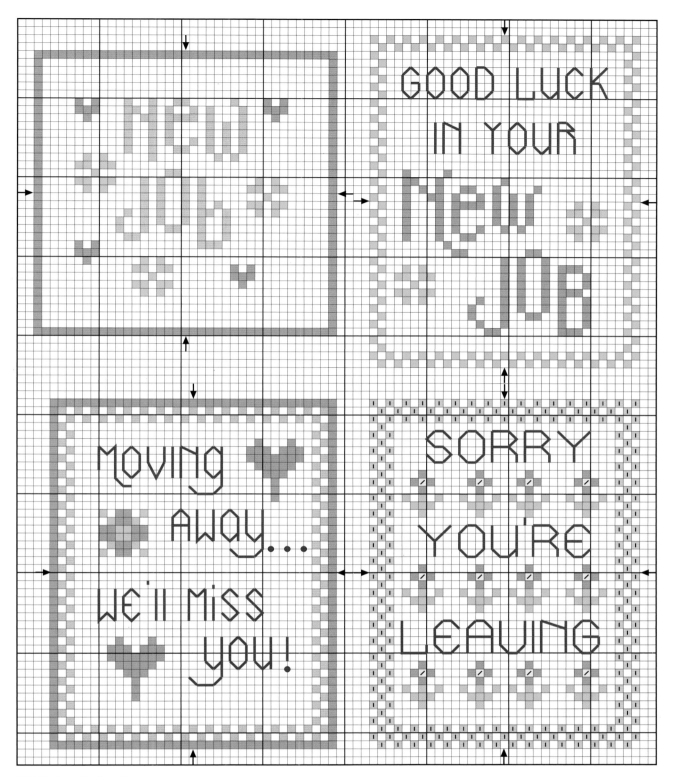

DMC stranded cotton

Cross stitch (2 strands)   Backstitch (1 strand)   French knots (2 strands)

▨ 340	▨ 742	— 797
▣ 352	▨ 3348	
▨ 677	▨ 3836	

● 797

Mini sampler

RETIREMENT
GIVES YOU
TIME TO GROW

SEEDS

NEW HOME

RETIREMENT

DMC stranded cotton

Cross stitch (2 strands)

■ 310	437	**I** 554	954
316	472	**–** 744	3347
317	552	**/** 842	3608

3822	**∧** Color Variations 4120
✗ ecru	
• blanc	**V** Color Variations 4230

Backstitch (1 strand)

— 310   — 552

— 317   — 3347

French knots (2 strands)

● 317

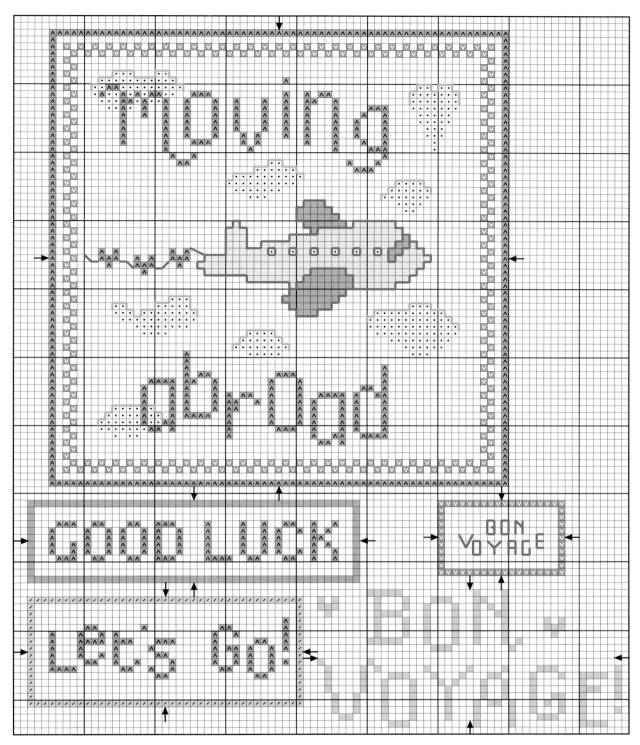

DMC stranded cotton

Cross stitch (2 strands)

✎ 598

3846

▲ Color Variations 4120

809

• blanc

▼ Color Variations 4230

3753

Backstitch (1 strand)

— 317

— 809

FRIENDS FOREVER

Stitching for friends is a real pleasure as we know their tastes and how thrilled they will be to receive our handmade gifts. To celebrate the joys of friendship this chapter has a delightful friends sampler with a charming little stuffed beehive scissor keeper to accompany it. Sometimes it's important to send our support and love to help friends through difficult or stressful times and there's a set of really special Friendship Affirmations hanging ornaments, which are just gorgeous both to stitch and receive. Get creative and decorate them with all kinds of ribbons, beads, charms and buttons.

Beehive Scissor Keeper

Stitch count: 42h x 33w

Design size: 7.6 x 6cm (3 x 2½in)

The bee button on this scissor keeper is optional but does add a fun finishing touch. You could also use the design as a key keeper. Stitch it over two threads of white 28-count linen using the chart on page 76. See page 99 for making up.

Friends Sampler

Stitch count: 119h x 66w

Design size: 21.5 x 12cm (8½ x 4¾in)

Fabric: 28-count pale pink linen (or 14-count Aida)

Threads: DMC stranded cotton (floss) listed in chart key

Embellishments: Bee button

Prepare your fabric for work. Follow the chart on page 72 and work over two linen threads (or one Aida block), using two strands of stranded cotton for full and three-quarter cross stitches and French knots and one strand for backstitches. Sew on the button with matching thread. Frame your sampler (see page 94).

Craft a Keepsake...

♥ Create mini samplers with smaller designs, such as the Best Friend chart on page 76.

♥ Use the Sew chart on page 77 to stitch a little scissor fob.

♥ Make a needle book by stitching the Needles chart on page 77 and adding squares of felt for the needlebook 'pages'.

♥ Make a card by stitching the Friends Forever chart on page 73. Back the stitching with fusible web, glue to a blank card and decorate with embellishments.

♥ Use the Stitching Friends chart on page 77 and make it up as a cushion, with a floral fabric border.

What friend wouldn't be delighted to receive this lovely sampler with its heartfelt message? You could also make the design up as a bolster cushion. The friends figures could be stitched alone for a small card.

Friendship Affirmations

What better way to show your affection for a friend than to stitch one of these charming hangings? You could stitch all three hangings to complete this cheerful saying, or choose the most suitable words of encouragement for the recipient. The designs make lovely gifts and are fun to embellish with beads and buttons. The curly wire handles can be decorated with scraps of ribbon and odds and ends of beads.

Craft a Keepsake . . .

♥ Choose your own affirmation to personalize your hanger.

♥ Stitch a hanger in your friend's favourite colours.

♥ Add sprigs of lavender or dried rose petals to the filling for a special touch.

Affirmation Wishes

Stitch count: 53h x 53w

Design size: 9.5 x 9.5cm (3¾ x 3¾in)

Fabric: 28-count linen in sand, pale pink, white or pale blue (or 14-count Aida)

Threads: DMC stranded cotton (floss) listed in chart key

Embellishments: Beads, buttons and ribbons

Prepare your fabric for work. Follow the chart on pages 74–75 and work over two linen threads (or one Aida block), using two strands of stranded cotton for cross stitches and one for backstitches. Sew on the beads and buttons using matching thread and then make up as described on page 100.

Sometimes we need to give extra support to a friend facing life's challenges, and this Be Brave design helps to express that loving encouragement, showing a friend we are there to help.

Mini sampler

DMC stranded cotton
Cross stitch (2 strands)

⁄ 209	351	471	∨ 760	3608		
317	╲ 352	I 676	958	• ecru		
340	437	744	⊙ 3607			

Backstitch (1 strand)

— 317
— 333

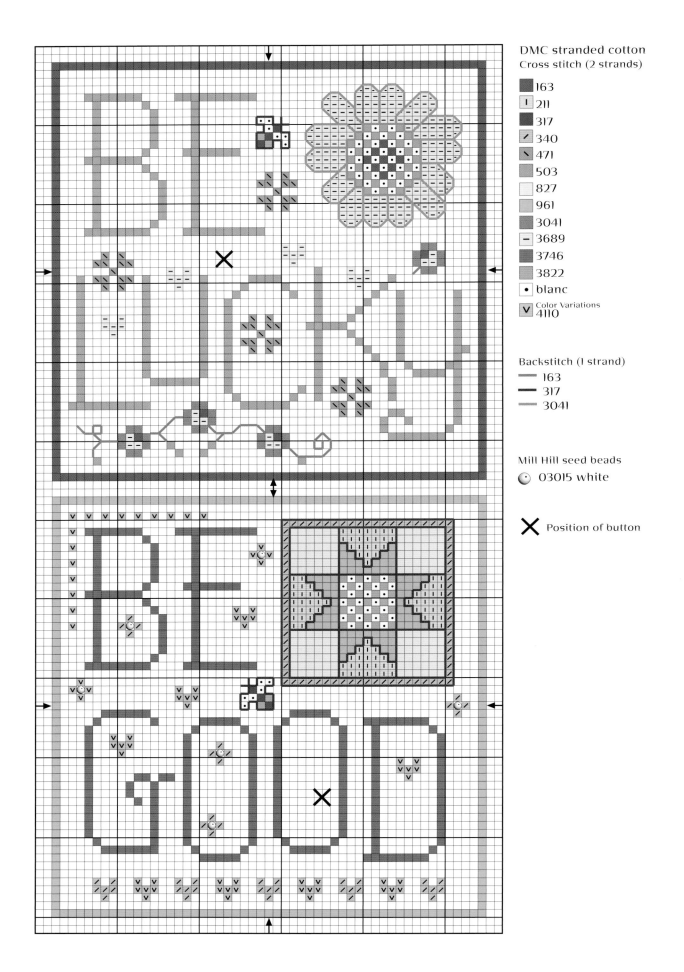

DMC stranded cotton
Cross stitch (2 strands)

163
I 211
317
✓ 340
\ 471
503
827
961
3041
– 3689
3746
3822
• blanc
V Color Variations
4110

Backstitch (1 strand)
—— 163
—— 317
—— 3041

Mill Hill seed beads
⊙ 03015 white

✕ Position of button

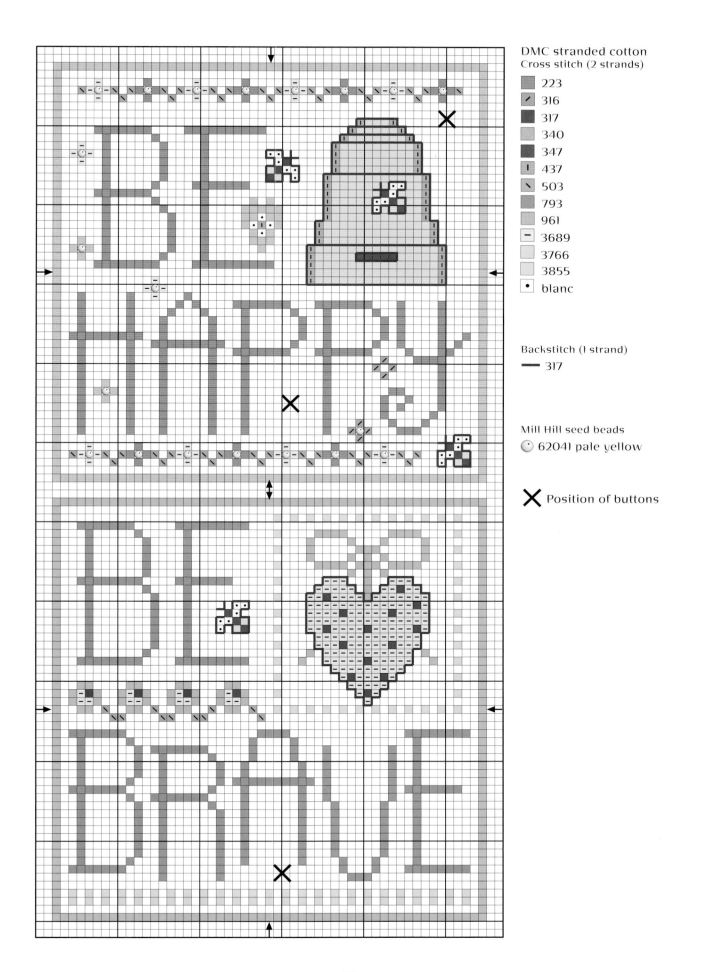

DMC stranded cotton
Cross stitch (2 strands)

▨	223
◤	316
■	317
▨	340
▨	347
▮	437
◥	503
▨	793
▨	961
−	3689
▨	3766
▨	3855
⊡	blanc

Backstitch (1 strand)
—— 317

Mill Hill seed beads
◉ 62041 pale yellow

✕ Position of buttons

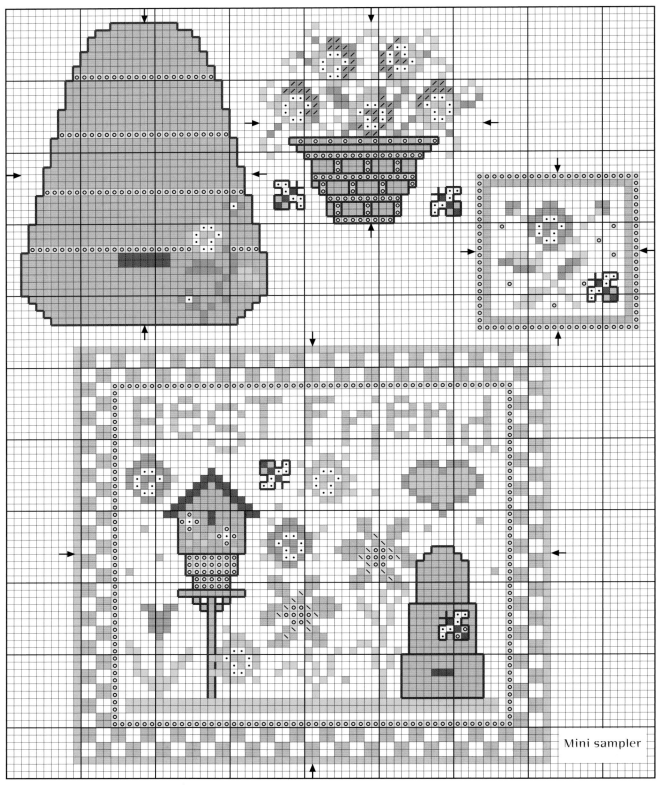

DMC stranded cotton
Cross stitch (2 strands)

■ 317	○ 676	■ 3348	■ 3832
■ 340	■ 729	╱ 3607	• blanc
╲ 341	■ 3347	■ 3608	

Backstitch (1 strand)
—— 317

Mini sampler

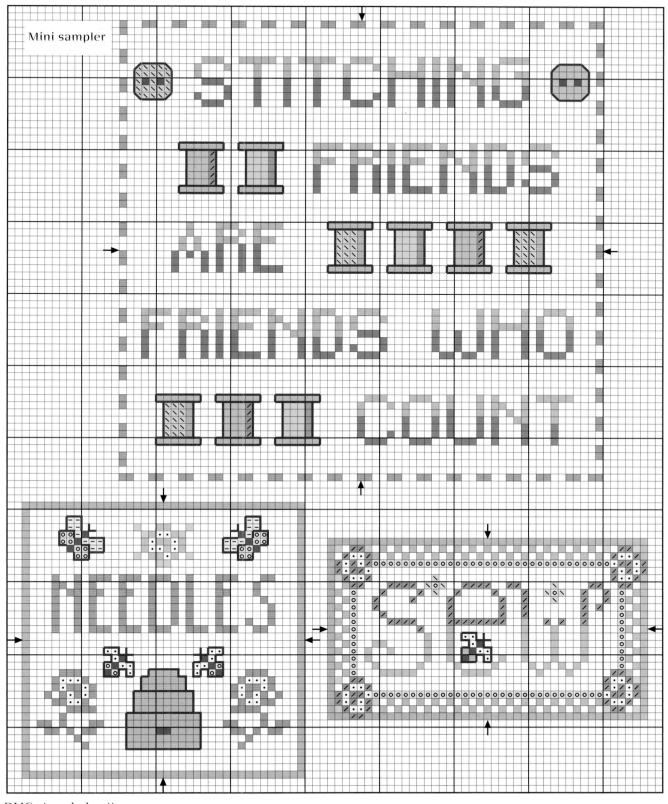

DMC stranded cotton
Cross stitch (2 strands)

■ 317	◉ 676	■ 3347	■ 3608	• blanc	
■ 340	■ 729	■ 3348	■ 3832		
＼ 341	− 827	╱ 3607	■ 3838		

Backstitch (1 strand)
—— 317

HOME AND FAMILY

Every stitcher loves to make things for their home and family, and there is plenty of choice in this chapter. A home sampler reminds us that family life is about sharing our lives, our love and our possessions. It's also nice to create something special for just one person, so there are designs for various family members. Why not make a coffee bean bag for Dad? A cookie jar for Grandpa could be used for other delicious goodies and re-labelled. Overleaf there are more homely gifts for the family, including some gorgeous girly treats. Charted designs also allow you to create lots of cards, including some for Mother's Day and Father's Day.

Coffee Crazy Bag and Tag

Stitch count: 30h x 24w
Design size: 5.5 x 4.5cm (2⅛ x 1¾in)

This stylish bag is fun to make – why not make one for tea bags using the Tea for Two design on page 85? Before you start, see page 101 for beginning the project, fabric sizes needed and where to position the motif. Use the chart on page 85, working only the coffee pot over two strands of 28-count sand linen. Sew on two heart buttons and see page 101 for making up.

To make a Coffee Crazy tag, use the chart on page 85 and white 28-count linen. See page 100 for making up.

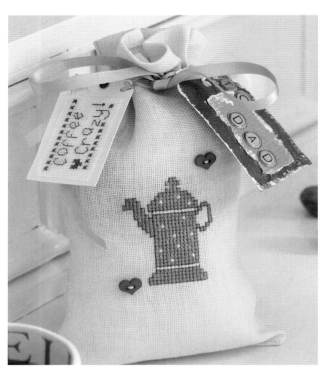

Home Sampler

Stitch count: 92h x 92w
Design size: 16.7 x 16.7cm (6½ x 6½in)
Fabric: 28-count white linen (or 14-count Aida)
Threads: DMC stranded cotton (floss) listed in chart key

Prepare your fabric for work. Follow the chart on page 82 and work over two linen threads (or one Aida block), using two strands of stranded cotton for cross stitch and one for backstitch. When complete, press and frame your sampler.

Craft a Keepsake. . .

♥ Make a fun hanger by stitching Welcome to My Shed from page 86 on to cream perforated paper. Cut out, glue it to stiff card and attach a wire or raffia hanger.

♥ Stitch the Happy Birthday design on page 86 to create a special birthday card for a much-loved brother.

♥ Create a beautiful card for Mother's Day using the design on page 89, and decorate it with floral embellishments.

♥ Make a cover for a gardening notebook with the Dad's Garden design on page 86.

This charming Home Sampler reminds us that it is at home that we learn to share our affections and possessions. Send love to family members with thoughtful gifts, such as a coffee bean bag for Dad and a cookie jar for Grandpa. Stitch the label and tag from page 87 and attach to the tag card and glass jar with double-sided tape.

Homely Gifts

Pamper and indulge the ones you love with some gorgeous gifts and create a fabulous welcome to your home and family with a decorated twiggy heart. There's also a pretty treat bag for a Divine Daughter – fill it with sweets or other surprises. For Mum, stitch a beautiful rose patchwork bag and add her favourite beauty products.

Divine Daughter Bag

Stitch count: 64h x 68w

Design size: 11.5 x 12.3cm (4½ x 4¾in)

Any daughter is sure to appreciate this lovely bag, and its sentiment. Add a glittery charm of your choice (see Suppliers). Before you start, refer to page 101 for beginning the project, the fabric sizes needed and the position of the cross stitch. Follow the chart on page 88 and work over two threads of 28-count pale pink linen. See page 101 for making up.

Heart and Home Wreath

Stitch count: 49h x 39w each pillow

Design size: 9 x 7cm (3½ x 2¾in)

Fabric: 28-count white linen

Threads: DMC stranded cotton (floss) listed in chart key

Embellishments: Various tiny buttons (see Suppliers)

Stitch the pillow designs on individual pieces of linen, using the charts on pages 83–84 and working over two threads. When stitching is complete, sew on the buttons and see page 98 for making up the pillows and wreath.

To make the little teapot, use the chart on page 88 and stitch over two threads of white 28-count linen. See page 99 for making up.

These little pillows with look wonderful displayed on a twiggy heart. You could also hang them individually or attach them to a larger gift. The little teapot pillow makes a charming addition.

Vintage Rose Bag and Tag

Stitch count: 18h x 21w for each rose motif

Design size: 3.2 x 3.8cm (1¼ x 1½in)

This gorgeous bag is the perfect gift for any female in the family – simply change the name on the tag. Before you start, refer to page 102 for beginning the project and the fabric sizes needed. Stitch the rose from page 89 in the centre of ten linen squares. See page 102 for making up.

For the Time for Me tag, follow the chart on page 85 and stitch over two threads of 28-count aqua linen. Sew on the flower button and see page 100 for making up. Stitch the Mum tag using the chart on page 87 and see page 100 for making up.

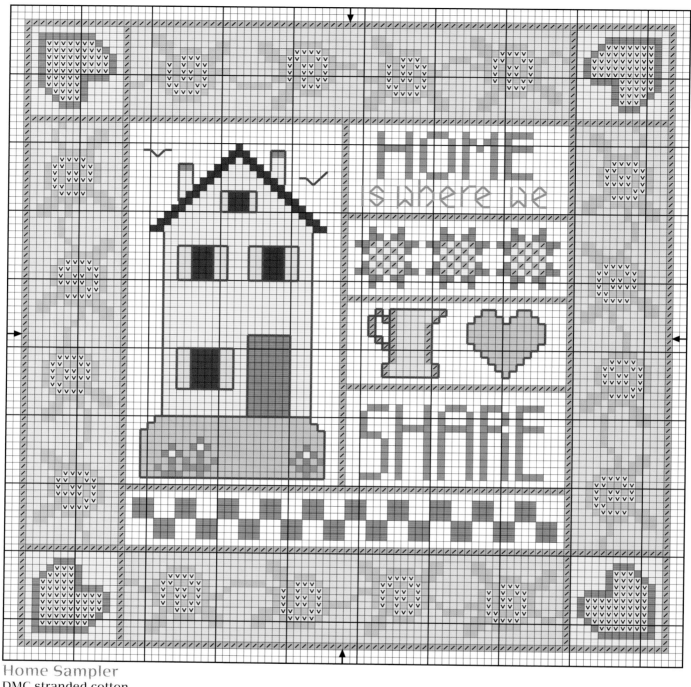

Home Sampler
DMC stranded cotton
Cross stitch (2 strands)

Backstitch (1 strand)

◼ 317	◻ 677	◼ 3833	✓ Color Variations 4170
◼ 502	◻ 800	◼ 3838	
◻ 563	◼ 3832	✓ 3839	

— 317

— 3838

DMC stranded cotton
Cross stitch (2 strands)

L 223	341	**I** 437	704	793	**O** 3832
317	**T** 415	503	**−** 747	956	**•** blanc
⟍ 340	436	677	761	**⁄** 3689	

Backstitch (1 strand)

— 316
— 317
— blanc

DMC stranded cotton
Cross stitch (2 strands)

T 156	**** 340	677	956	**o** 3832
316	341	761	**/** 3689	**I** 3838
317	503	**^** 807	**–** 3766	**·** blanc

Backstitch (1 strand)

— 317
— 437
— 503
═ blanc

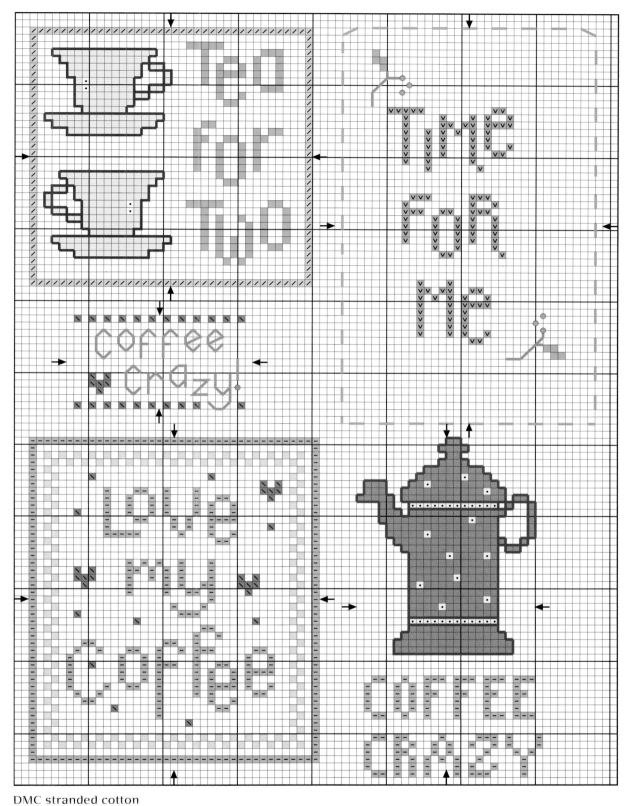

DMC stranded cotton

Cross stitch (2 strands)

⁄ 341	3046	3861
503	3716	• blanc
- 642	3860	v Color Variations 4020

Backstitch (1 strand)

— 317   — 3860

— 502   — 3861

— 3832

French knots (2 strands)

● 3832

● 3861

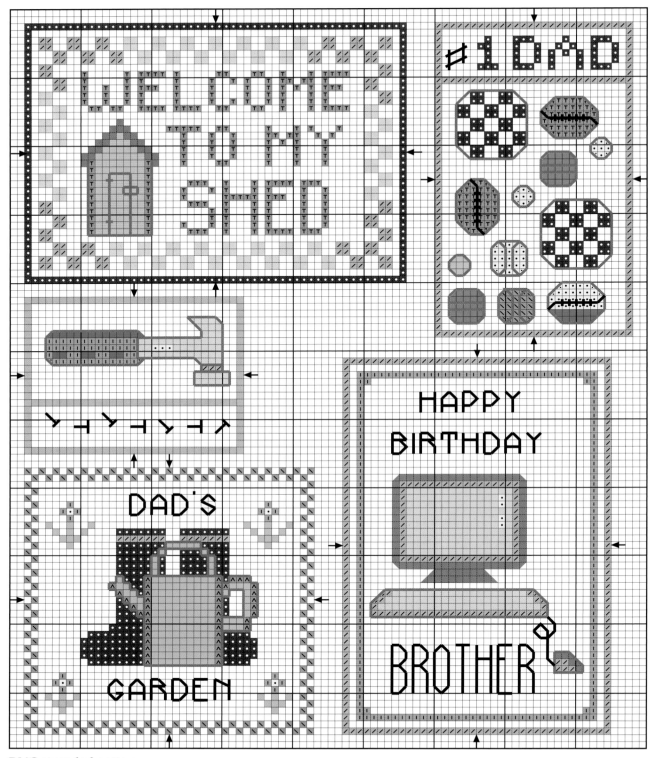

DMC stranded cotton

Cross stitch (2 strands)

◼ 310	✦ 318	437	▮ 826	3045
312	349	◥ 503	⋀ 906	• ecru
317	415	598	907	

Backstitch (1 strand)

— 310

— 317

DMC stranded cotton
Backstitch (1 strand)

—— 310

—— 3832

Color Variations
—— 4020

French knots (2 strands)

● 310

DMC stranded cotton

Cross stitch (2 strands)

340	704	3839
437	956	
677	3608	

Backstitch (1 strand)

317

3839

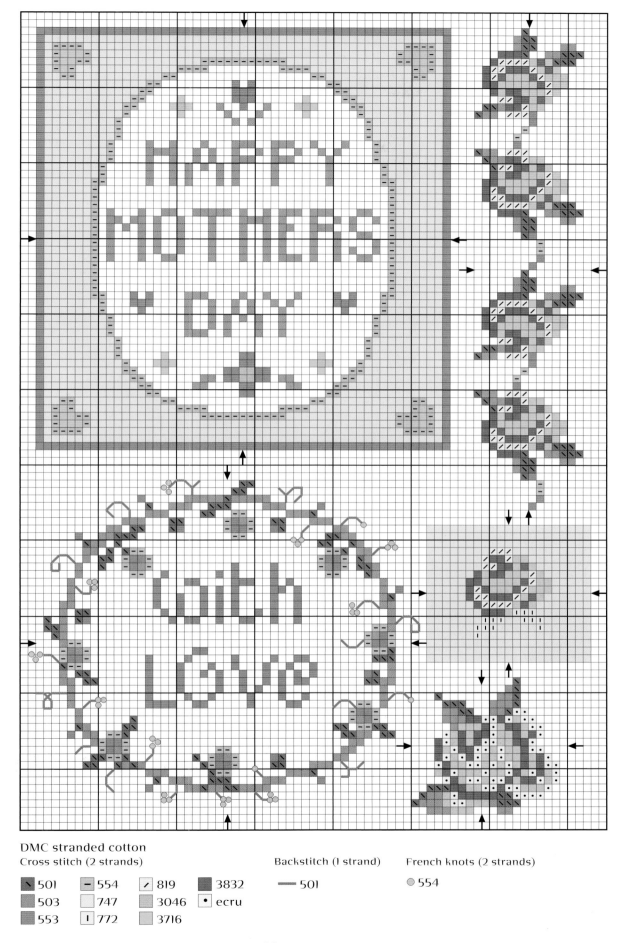

DMC stranded cotton

Cross stitch (2 strands)

■ 501	– 554	✓ 819	■ 3832
■ 503	747	3046	• ecru
■ 553	I 772	3716	

Backstitch (1 strand)

—— 501

French knots (2 strands)

◉ 554

MATERIALS AND TECHNIQUES

This section should be particularly useful to beginners as it contains information on the materials and equipment you will need and the basic techniques needed to work the projects in the book. Refer to Suppliers for useful addresses.

Materials

Fabrics
The designs have been worked on a blockweave fabric called Aida and on evenweave or linen fabrics. If working on Aida, stitch over one block; if working on evenweave stitch over two fabric threads. If you change the gauge (count) of the material, that is the number of holes per inch, then the size of the finished work will alter accordingly. See right for working out stitch counts and finished design sizes.

Threads
The projects have been stitched with DMC stranded embroidery cotton (floss) but you could match the colours to other thread ranges – ask at your local needlework store. The six-stranded skeins can easily be split into separate strands. The project instructions and charts tell you how many strands to use. Some projects use variegated thread for subtle shaded effects.

Needles
Tapestry needles, available in different sizes, are used for cross stitch as they have a rounded point and do not snag fabric. You will need a thinner beading needle to attach the small glass seed beads used in some of the projects.

Frames
It is a matter of personal preference as to whether you use an embroidery frame to keep your fabric taut while stitching. Generally speaking, working with a frame helps to keep the tension even and prevent distortion, while working without a frame is faster and less cumbersome. There are various types on the market – look in your local needlework store for some examples.

Techniques

Stitch Count and Design Size
All the motifs and charts in this book were designed to fit 14-count Aida or 28-count linen or evenweave fabric. You can stitch the designs on fabric with a lower or higher count than this as long as you are aware that it will change the finished size of the design. Being able to calculate the eventual size of a design means that you can decide how much fabric you need for a particular project or whether a design will fit a specific picture frame or card aperture.

To work out the stitch count, first count how many stitches there are along the height of a design and then along the width (don't forget to count backstitches and French knots too on the outer edge of a design). The illustration below shows a design that is 22 stitches high and 22 stitches wide.

To work out the finished design size, divide each of the stitch count numbers by the fabric count of the embroidery fabric you want to use. For example, the charted design below is 22 high x 22 wide and the fabric is 14-count Aida. So, 22 ÷ 14 = 1.57, which is more or less 1½ inches, both ways. So the stitched design will be 1½in (3.8cm) square. The same design worked on 18-count Aida would have a smaller finished size of 1¼in (3.2cm) square, because 18-count fabric is finer.

When calculating design sizes for evenweave fabrics, divide the fabric count by 2 before you start, because evenweave is worked over two threads not one block as with Aida.

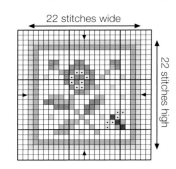

Counting stitches across the height and width of a charted design

Preparing the Fabric

Spending a little time preparing your embroidery fabric before stitching will save time and trouble in the long run.

♥ Before starting work, check the design size given with each project and make sure that this is the size you require for your finished embroidery. Your fabric must be larger than the finished design size to allow for making up, so allow 13cm (5in) to both dimensions when stitching a sampler and 7.5cm (3in) for smaller projects.

♥ Before beginning to stitch, neaten the fabric edges either by hemming or zigzagging to prevent fraying as you work. If using plastic canvas, neaten all the edges by trimming off any sharp or rough pieces to avoid snagging thread.

♥ Find the centre of the fabric. This is important regardless of which direction you work from, in order to stitch the design centrally on the fabric. To find the centre, fold the fabric in half horizontally and then vertically, then tack (baste) along the folds (or use tailor's chalk). The centre point is where the two lines of tacking meet. This point on the fabric should correspond to the centre point on the chart. Remove these lines on completion of the work.

Using Charts and Keys

The charts in this book are easy to work from. Each square represents one stitch. Each coloured square, or coloured square with a symbol, represents a thread colour, with the code number given in the chart key. A few of the designs use fractional stitches (three-quarter stitches) to give more definition. Solid coloured lines show where backstitches or long stitches are to be worked. French knots are shown by coloured circles. Larger coloured circles with a dot indicate beads. Each complete chart has arrows at the side to show the centre point, which you could mark with a pen.

Caring for Finished Work

Cross stitch embroidery can be washed and ironed, though care should be taken with delicate ceramic buttons. Make sure it is colourfast first, then wash with bleach-free soap in hand-hot water, squeezing gently but never rubbing or wringing. Rinse in cold or lukewarm water and dry naturally.

To iron cross stitch embroidery, use a hot setting on a steam iron. Cover the ironing board with thick towels and place the stitching on this, right side down. Press the fabric firmly but avoid charms, buttons and metallic threads.

Starting and Finishing

It is always a good idea to start and finish work correctly, to create the neatest effect and avoid ugly bumps and threads trailing across the back of work. To finish off thread, pass the needle through several nearby stitches on the wrong side of the work, then cut the thread off, close to the fabric.

Knotless Loop Start

Starting this way can be very useful with stranded cotton (floss), but only works if you are intending to stitch with an even number of threads, i.e. 2, 4, or 6. Cut the stranded cotton roughly twice the length you would normally need and separate one strand. Double this strand and thread your needle with the two ends. Pierce your fabric from the wrong side where you intend to place your first stitch, leaving the looped end at the back of the work. Return your needle to the wrong side after forming a half cross stitch and pass the needle through the waiting loop. You can now begin to stitch.

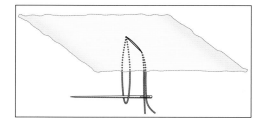

Fig 1 Beginning stitching with a knotless loop

Away Waste Knot Start

Start this way if working with an odd number of strands or when using variegated threads. Thread your needle and make a knot at the end. Take the needle and thread through from the front of the fabric to the back and come up again about 2.5cm (1in) away from the knot. Now either start cross stitching and work towards the knot, cutting it off when the threads are anchored, or thread the end into your needle and finish off under some completed stitches.

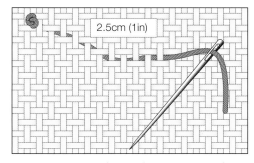

Fig 2 Beginning stitching with an away waste knot

Working the Stitches

There are no complicated stitches to master and all of those used within the projects are described here, accompanied by diagrams.

Algerian Eye

This is a star-like stitch that can have different numbers of radiating stitches. You can also vary the length of the 'arms' to create different shapes.

Following the diagram below, work in the same direction around each stitch, always passing the needle down through the central hole.

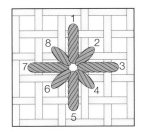

Fig 3 Algerian eye or star stitch

Backstitch

Backstitch (and long stitch) is indicated on the charts by a solid coloured line. It can be worked on its own for lettering, on top of other stitches for detail and as an outline around areas of completed cross stitches to add definition. Most backstitch is worked with one strand of thread.

To work backstitch, bring the needle up through the fabric at 1 (see diagram below), then take it down at 2. Bring it up at 3 and then down at 4 and so on. This produces short stitches on the front of the work and longer ones on the back.

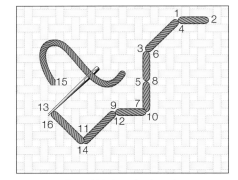

Fig 4 Working backstitch

Cross Stitch

This is the main stitch used throughout the projects and each complete cross stitch is represented on the charts by a coloured square. The cross stitches in this book are worked over two threads of evenweave (linen) or one block of Aida.

A cross stitch is worked in two stages: a diagonal stitch is worked over two threads (or one block), then a second diagonal stitch is worked over the first stitch in the opposite direction, forming a cross (see Fig 5a and 5b below).

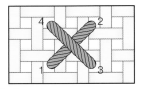

Fig 5a A single cross stitch on Aida

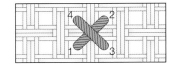

Fig 5b A single cross stitch on evenweave

If you have a large area to cover, you could work the cross stitches in two journeys, in rows. Work a row of half cross stitches in one direction, then work back in the opposite direction with the diagonal stitches needed to complete each cross stitch (see Fig 6a and 6b). The upper stitches of all the crosses should lie in the same direction to produce a neat effect.

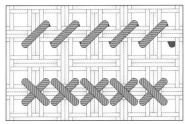

Fig 6a Cross stitch worked in two journeys on Aida

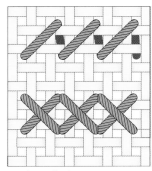

Fig 6b Cross stitch worked in two journeys on evenweave

Three-quarter Cross Stitch

This is a part or fractional stitch that is useful for adding detail to a design and creating smoother curves or circles. Three-quarter cross stitch is shown on the charts by a coloured triangle within a square.

To work three-quarter cross stitch, work a half cross stitch, then add a quarter stitch in the opposite direction, bringing the needle down in the centre of the half cross stitch already worked (see Fig 7).

Fig 7 Three-quarter cross stitch

French Knot

This is a useful little stitch and may be used in addition to cross stitch to add texture and emphasis. In this book they are usually worked with two strands of thread wound once around the needle, and are shown on the charts by a small coloured circle.

To work a French knot, bring the needle up to the right side of the fabric, hold the thread down with your left thumb (if right-handed) and wind the thread around the needle twice (see diagram below). Still holding the thread taut, put the needle through to the back of the work, one thread or part of a block away from the entry point. If you want bigger knots, add more thread to the needle.

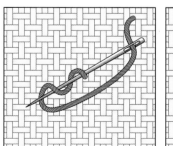

Fig 8 Working a French knot

Attaching Beads

Attach beads using a beading needle or very fine 'sharp' needle. Use thread that matches the bead colour and secure with either a half cross stitch or a full cross stitch.

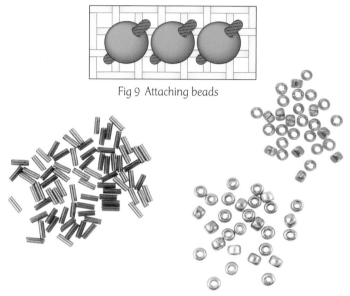

Fig 9 Attaching beads

Tips for Perfect Stitching

Cross stitch is a simple stitch and easy to do but your work will look its best if you follow these guides.

- ♥ Wash your hands before beginning stitching, and use hand cream to keep them smooth.
- ♥ Always work in a good light, near a window during the day or with a special 'daylight' lamp at night.
- ♥ Use the knotless loop method (page 91) to start your stitching – it stops knots spoiling the surface.
- ♥ If stitching with variegated thread use a waste knot start (page 91).
- ♥ Make sure that your cross stitches all have the top stitches facing in the same direction.
- ♥ Don't pull the thread too tight – be gentle and consistent and the result will be more professional.
- ♥ If you find it difficult to stitch accurately, especially backstitch, use an embroidery hoop.
- ♥ To prevent thread becoming tangled, 'drop' the needle occasionally to allow the thread to untwist.
- ♥ Sort your spare threads on to bobbins and store neatly in boxes or drawers – it will save time when you search for specific threads later.
- ♥ Tidy your work away in a cotton bag, or if it is a large piece on a frame cover it with an old sheet to protect from dust and marks.

MAKING UP

The projects have been made up in lots of lovely ways and other suggestions are offered throughout the chapters. The techniques are explained over the following pages, beginning with general ones, followed by some specific methods used.

Mounting and Framing Your Embroidery

It really is best to take large samplers and pictures to a professional framer, where you can choose from a wide variety of mounts and frames that will best enhance your work. The framer will be able to lace and stretch the fabric correctly and cut mounts accurately. They can also cut mounts into more unusual shapes, such as ovals.

If you intend to stretch and mount the work yourself, use acid-free mounting board in a colour that will not show through the embroidery. Cut the board to fit inside your picture frame and allow for the thickness of the fabric pulled over the edges of the board. There are two common methods used for stretching an embroidery over a mount board – taping and lacing.

Taping Method

Place the cut board on the reverse of the work in the position required. Starting from the centre of one of the longest edges, fold the fabric over the board and pin through the fabric into the edge of the board to keep the fabric from moving. Check it is in the correct place with no wrinkles or bumps, then stick the work in place using strips of double-sided adhesive tape, removing the pins once stretching is finished.

Lacing Method

Pin the work in place on the board, as described above, and then working from the centre and using long lengths of very strong thread, such as linen or buttonhole thread, lace backwards and forwards across the gap. Repeat for the shorter sides, taking care to mitre or fold the corners in neatly. Remove pins once finished.

Mounting Work into Ready-made Items

There are many ready-made items specially made for displaying embroidery, including notebooks, coasters, rulers, pen holders, fridge magnets, key rings, name plates and babies' bibs. Mount your work into these items following the manufacturer's instructions. Use a piece of paper or thin card to hide the back of any stitching that may be seen. It also helps to back the stitched design with iron-on interfacing to add stiffness and prevent fabric fraying (see opposite).

Mounting Work into Cards

There are many lovely card mounts available today. Double-fold cards are pre-folded with three sections, the middle one having a window for your embroidery.

1 First make sure your embroidery looks good in the window space, then trim your design to the correct size – it needs to be at least 2.5cm (1in) larger than the aperture on all sides.

2 Position lengths of double-sided adhesive tape around the window area then remove the backing from the tape. (Note: some cards already have this tape in place.) Lay the card on top of the embroidery so that it shows neatly through the window and press into place.

3 Fold the third of the card to cover the back of the embroidery, ensuring that the card opens correctly before securing with more tape.

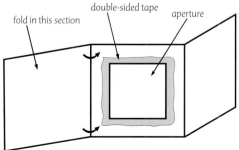

double-sided tape

fold in this section   aperture

Positioning the embroidery in the card aperture

Using Iron-on Interfacing and Adhesive Webbing

Iron-on interfacing can be used to stiffen and stabilize your cross stitch embroidery and allow the edges to be cut without fraying. Cut the interfacing to size and fuse it to the back of the finished embroidery with a medium iron, with the embroidery face down on some thick towels.

Adhesive webbing is available as single-sided and double-sided, i.e., with glue on one side or both, allowing you to fuse the embroidery to another fabric. This means that you can use your cross stitch to decorate all sorts of ready-made items, such as bags, nightdress cases, even teddy bears! The webbing is also fused to the embroidery by means of a medium iron.

Baby Stars

1 When cross stitching is complete, cut a square of backing fabric the same size and place the pieces right sides together. Sew round the star and then make a small opening in the centre of the back. Cut round the star shape and turn out to the right side.

2 Press the star, fill with stuffing and over sew the opening. Attach a ribbon hanger to the top.

Sew around the two star shapes. Turn through to the right side and sew up the gap.

Baby's First Christmas

1 When cross stitching is complete, cut a square of backing fabric the same size and place the pieces right sides together. Sew round the shape leaving a small gap at the bottom. Turn through to the right side, stuff the shape and over sew the gap.
2 Attach a length of red ribbon for a hanging loop and sew small bells along the bottom.

Valentine Heart

1 When cross stitching is complete, cut a piece of backing fabric the same size and place right sides together with the embroidery. Sew around the heart shape leaving a small gap at the top.
2 Cut out the heart shape to within about 1.25cm (½in) of the stitching, clip the curves and turn through to the right side. Stitch up the gap, inserting a length of narrow ribbon for hanging at the same time. Make a bead tassel with two pearl beads and a drop bead and sew to the heart.

Teddy Toys

1 When cross stitching is complete, do not cut out the toy shape until you have stitched it together. First sew on the buttons very securely (especially if the toy is for a young child). Trace the template on page 103 on to a sheet of paper and cut out. Place the front and back pieces right sides together and sew around the toy shape (see diagram below). Trim off excess fabric to within about 1.25cm (½in) of the stitched line. Make a small opening in the centre of the back and turn right way out. Press, stuff firmly with polyester stuffing and then over sew the opening in the back.
2 To make the face, use double-sided iron-on interfacing (see page 95) to iron on a triangle of blue fabric for a nose. For eyes, use a large pin head pressed on an ink pad. Sew a line of black backstitch for the mouth and brush on lipstick for cheeks. Tie on a gingham bow to finish.

Sewing the front and back pieces together following the toy shape

Sweetheart Box

There are many boxes available with lids that allow the insertion of cross stitch designs – see Debbie Cripps in Suppliers. The Keepsake Boxes on page 12 can be treated the same way.

1 Make sure the stitching will fit the lid aperture by comparing it to the finished design size of the stitching. When stitching is complete paint the box in your chosen colour using craft or emulsion paints. Allow to dry thoroughly.

2 Iron fusible web on to the back of the stitching. Cut out your design and insert it into the box lid.

Bottle Label

1 Measure the circumference of the bottle you wish the label to cover and cut a piece of linen to fit, allowing for a narrow seam and turnings at the top and bottom. Hem the top and bottom, and then find the centre of the fabric and stitch the charted design.

2 Press the stitching and then sew up the seam and slip the label over the bottle.

First Day Quilted Hanging

To make up the patchwork hanger on page 44 you will need: white cotton backing fabric, red and white gingham, fusible webbing, polyester wadding (batting), two mother-of-pearl buttons and a 30cm (12in) length of thick white cord.

1 Iron fusible webbing on to the back of the finished embroidery. Cut four strips of red gingham 4cm (1½in) wide, plus 2cm (¾in) for seam allowances and sew to the embroidery – side strips first and then top and bottom.

2 Take a piece of white backing fabric the same size as the bordered fabric and place the pieces right sides together. Sew together around the edges leaving a gap at the bottom to turn out. Turn right way out and press seams. Cut a piece of wadding slightly smaller than the hanging, place inside the hanging and sew up the gap.

3 Using white thread, make quilting (running) stitches around the sampler, and around the inner and outer edges of the gingham border. Sew on the buttons in the lower corners. Make a hole in the top left and right corners, thread the hanging cord through and tie the ends with a knot.

First Year Album

1 Stretch the finished stitching over the front cover of your album, fixing in place with double-sided tape. Turn the right-hand edge and the two top edges inside the cover, mitre the corners, and stick down.
2 Repeat this process with a matching piece of fabric for the back. Cut a smaller piece of fabric for the album spine, secure with double-sided tape. Fold and fix the top and bottom edges inside the cover.
3 Where the fabric pieces join, neaten the edges with strips of self-adhesive gingham ribbon, turning the ends inside the cover. Inside the album, neaten the front and back covers by gluing on pieces of decorative paper.

Alphabet Bag

To make up the bag on page 44 you will need: iron-on interfacing, blue and white striped cotton ticking, plain white fabric, pink flower buttons and polyester stuffing for the handles. The finished size of the bag is 17 x 21cm (6¾ x 8¼in).
1 Begin by ironing the interfacing on to the back of the embroidery and trim to size. Cut two pieces of ticking and two pieces of backing fabric. Cut two strips of white fabric 6cm (2³⁄₈in) wide and 22cm (8¾in) long for handles. Fold these in half lengthways and sew together to make a tube. Turn right side out, press and stuff the handles with polyester stuffing.
2 Cut two strips of white fabric 19 x 7cm (7½ x 2¾in) for the scalloped edging at the top. Draw around an egg cup to make the scallop shape and then sew round the shape with right sides together. Clip the corners, turn out and press.
3 Sew the two pieces of ticking right sides together and sew the white lining together. Insert into the bag with the scallop edging and the handles caught in between and then sew round, leaving a small opening for turning. Clip the corners, turn right side out and press.
4 Sew on the pink flower buttons.
Take the cross stitch initial patch, fray the edges a little, iron adhesive web on to the back and then iron the patch on the bag.

Wreath Pillows

1 Take the cross stitched front of the pillow and cut backing fabric the same size. With right sides together sew around the sides and top, leaving an opening at the bottom.
2 Clip the corners, turn the pillow the right way out and press. Stuff with polyester stuffing or scented pot-pourri and sew up the opening.
3 Attach the pillows to the wreath with safety pins or Velcro stick-on pads.

Study Buddies

To make up the toys on page 48 you will need: cotton fabric, polyester granules, polyester stuffing, white cotton-covered balls for heads, dolls' hair, string, button embellishments and a glue gun. The finished size of the small buddy is approximately 15 x 13cm (6 x 5¼in) and the large buddy is 26 x 15cm (10¼ x 6in).

Small Study Buddy

1 Take two pieces of checked cotton fabric 12 x 18cm (4¾ x 7in) and make a hem at the top of both pieces. With right sides together sew up the sides and along the bottom, trim seams, clip corners and turn right way out. Use adhesive webbing to fuse the embroidery to the body. Press and then fill the body with polyester granules. Thread string through the top hem, pull up tight and tie in a bow.

2 Take a cotton-covered ball and glue doll's hair to the top. Brush on lipstick for cheeks and dip a pin head in ink for eyes. Attach the head to the body using a glue gun. Sew on decorative buttons to finish.

Large Study Buddy

1 Take two pieces of striped cotton 20 x 18cm (7¾ x 7in) and follow step 1 above.
2 Make a frill for the collar by turning a 20cm (8in) strip of cotton fabric in half and running a thread through it. Pull it up to form the frill and glue in place with a glue gun.
3 Make a template for the arms from the pattern on page 103 and cut out of white cotton. With right sides together, sew round the outside of each arm leaving the top open. Clip curves, turn right way out and press. Stuff with polyester filling and close the opening. Slipstitch the arms to the sides of the body.
4 Follow step 2 above for making and attaching the head. Add embellishments of your choice.

Apple, Beehive and Teapot

These stuffed three-dimensional shapes are all made up in a similar way.
1 When cross stitching is complete, take some backing fabric the same size as the embroidered fabric and place right sides together. Sew round the shape leaving a small gap at the top.
2 Press the work and then cut around the shape carefully, about 6mm (¼in) from the stitching. Clip the curves and turn through to the right side. Stuff firmly with polyester stuffing and sew up the gap neatly.
3 Sew on any buttons being used, such as the bee button for the scissor keeper. If you need a length of cord, ribbon or twine for a hanger, insert this into the gap before closing. See page 102 for making your own twisted cord. Attach the Best Teacher label with a coloured safety pin and tie a bow around the hanging cord.

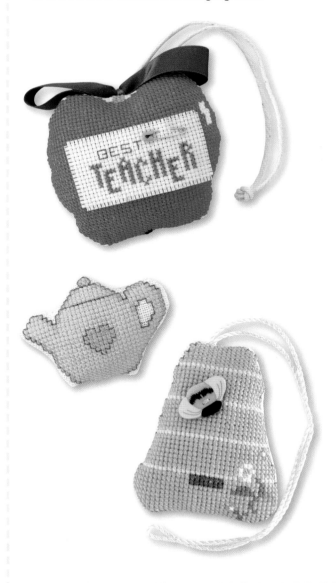

Affirmations Wishes

The Moving Abroad Hanger on page 60 is made in the same way. The Anniversary Hangings on page 34 are made similarly but with ribbon hanging loops instead of wire.

1 Follow step 1 of Baby's First Christmas, page 96.

2 Make a wire hanger using fine craft wire, cutting the wire to the length you want your hanger to be. Twist part of the wire by winding it round a pencil then sliding it off. Thread beads on to the untwisted side and tie on scraps of ribbon. Add charms or buttons of your choice. Bend each end of the wire into a small loop and secure to the back of the hanger with a few stitches.

Gift Tags

Good Luck Tag and Coffee Crazy Tag

The instructions apply to any stitched message or motif – simply change the sizes and embellishments as desired. The Bon Voyage tag on page 60 and the Mum tag on the Vintage Rose Bag on page 80 are made in a similar way.

1 Stitch your chosen motif or message and back the stitching with iron-on interfacing to help prevent edges fraying. Trim the stitching to the size required and glue it to a piece of decorative paper and then glue the mounted stitching on to a piece of stiff card.

2 Punch a hole in the top of the card, insert an eyelet if desired and thread thin ribbon or rustic string through.

Pen Pot

1 Measure the circumference of the pot you wish the label to cover and cut a piece of linen to fit, allowing for a narrow seam and turnings at the top and bottom. Hem the top and bottom, then find the fabric centre and stitch the charted design.

2 Once all stitching is complete, press and then sew up the seam. Slip the label over the pot.

Time for Me Tag

1 When stitching is complete, trim the fabric to size – about 2.5cm (1in) away from the stitching. Cut another piece of linen the same size. Place the pieces right sides together, sew all round, leaving a gap at the top for turning through.

2 Turn to the right side, stuff with polyester filling or pot-pourri and sew up the gap, inserting a loop of thin ribbon into the gap before closing.

Divine Daughter Bag

1 Begin with two pieces of 28-count pale pink linen 22 x 15cm (8½ x 6in). Press a hem at the top edges of both pieces using iron-on webbing or hemming stitches (see diagram). Stitch the motif on one of the linen pieces in the position shown on the diagram.

2 Withdraw six threads from both pieces of linen 3.2cm (1¼in) down from the top hem (for a channel for the ribbon tie). With right sides together sew up the sides of the bag and along the bottom, then trim the seams and clip the corners. Turn the bag right way out and press.

3 Thread thin ribbon through the drawn thread row. Fill the bag with treats, pull up the ribbon and tie in a bow. Add a sparkly charm to finish.

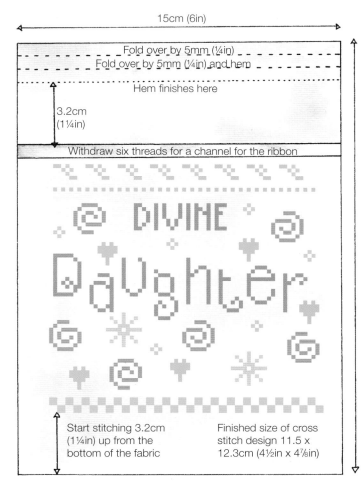

15cm (6in)

Fold over by 5mm (¼in)

Fold over by 5mm (¼in) and hem

Hem finishes here

3.2cm (1¼in)

Withdraw six threads for a channel for the ribbon

22cm (8½in)

Start stitching 3.2cm (1¼in) up from the bottom of the fabric

Finished size of cross stitch design 11.5 x 12.3cm (4½in x 4⅞in)

Coffee Crazy Bag

The finished size of this bag is 20 x 12cm (8 x 4¾in).

1 Begin with two pieces of 28-count sand linen 25 x 14cm (10 x 5½in). Hem the top of each piece. Stitch the motif in the centre of one of the linen pieces.

2 Refer to steps 2 and 3 for the Divine Daughter Bag, above, for making up and finishing the bag.

Vintage Rose Bag

To make the bag you will need: thirteen 7.5cm (3in) squares of 28-count aqua linen – this includes seam allowances of 1.25cm (½in) to make a 5cm (2in) finished square; fourteen 7.5cm (3in) squares of floral print fabric; two floral strips 12cm (30in) long x 7.6cm (3in) wide for handles and lining fabric.

1 Stitch the rose motif in the centre of each of ten of the linen squares (three are left plain).

2 Using the thirteen linen squares and fourteen floral squares assemble the patchwork as shown in the diagram below – stitch the squares together in rows and then stitch the rows together to make two patchwork pieces three squares high x four squares wide. For the base of the bag stitch the remaining three squares together and sew to the bottom of one of the larger patchwork pieces. Sew the other panel to the base, press the patchwork and then sew up the sides to create a bag shape.

3 Cut a piece of lining fabric the same size as the patchwork, create a bag shape the same as the patchwork and sew up the sides.

4 For handles, take two strips of floral fabric, place the strips right sides together and sew down the long sides with 1.25cm (½in) seams. Turn through to the right side and press the strip, then cut into two equal lengths. Pin the handles to each side of the patchwork as shown on the second diagram, facing inwards.

5 Place the lining fabric and patchwork right sides together and sew all round, catching the handles in the lining seam as you sew, and leaving a gap for turning out. Turn out and stitch up the gap, shaping the sides and bottom of the bag with the point of an iron.

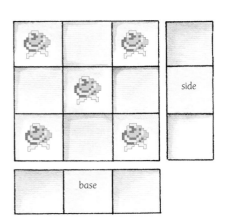

Joining the patchwork squares and assembling the bag

Making a Twisted Cord

A twisted cord can be used to embellish projects, to create a decorative edging and to make hanging loops. If you can't find a ready-made cord in the colour you need, it is simple to make your own from stranded cottons or other embroidery threads.

1 Choose a colour or group of colours in stranded cottons (or other threads) to match the embroidery.

2 Cut a minimum of four lengths at least four times the finished length required and fold in half. Ask a friend to hold the two ends while you slip a pencil through the loop at the other end. Twist the pencil and continue twisting until kinks appear. Walk slowly towards your partner and the cord will twist.

3 Smooth out the kinks from the looped end and secure with a knot at the other end.

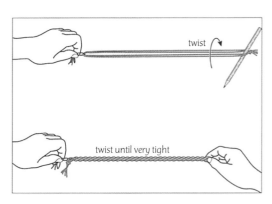

Making a length of twisted cord from embroidery threads

Templates

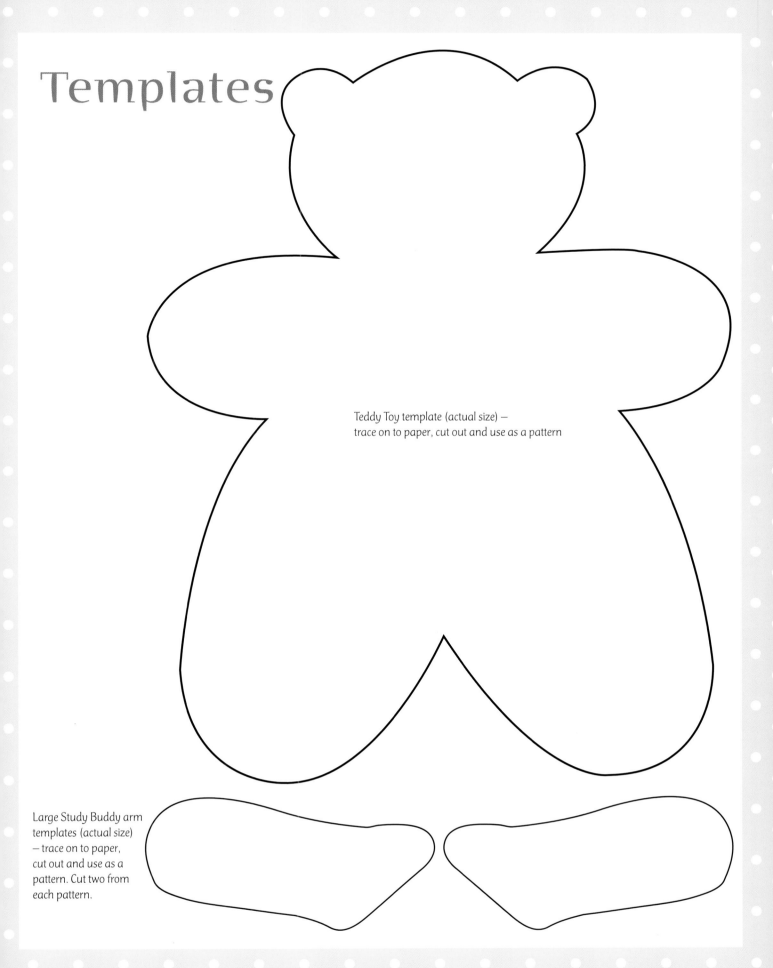

Teddy Toy template (actual size) –
trace on to paper, cut out and use as a pattern

Large Study Buddy arm
templates (actual size)
– trace on to paper,
cut out and use as a
pattern. Cut two from
each pattern.

Suppliers

UK

Coats Crafts UK
PO Box 22, Lingfield House, McMullen Road,
Darlington, County Durham DL1 1YQ
Tel: 01325 394237 (consumer helpline)
www.coatscrafts.co.uk
*For Anchor stranded cotton (floss) and other
embroidery supplies*

Courtyard Crafts
Brimstage Hall, Wirral CH63 6JA
Tel: 0151 342 4216
www.courtyardcrafts.co.uk
*Card embellishments, blank cards,
scrapbook supplies*

Debbie Cripps
8 Christchurch Street, West Frome,
Somerset BA11 1EQ
Tel: 01373 454448
www.debbiecripps.co.uk
*For aperture boxes, beads, buttons, charms
and many other supplies (the Divine
Daughter Bag uses a card charm)*

Dee Fine Arts
182 Telegraph Road, Heswall,
Wirral CH60 0AJ
Tel: 0151 342 6657
For expert embroidery and picture framing

DMC Creative World
Pullman Road, Wigston, Leicestershire
LE18 2DY
Tel: 0116 281 1040
www.dmccreative.co.uk
*For stranded cottons, metallic threads,
embroidery fabrics and other supplies*

Framecraft Miniatures Ltd
Unit 3, Isis House, Lindon Road,
Brownhills, West Midlands WS8 7BW
Tel/Fax (UK): 01543 360842
Tel (International): 44 1543 45315
www.framecraft.com
*For wooden trinket bowls and boxes,
notebook covers, pincushions, bookmarks
and many other pre-finished items with
cross stitch inserts*

Fred Aldous
Tel: 0161 236 4224
www.fredaldous.co.uk
*Craft materials, including doll making
supplies and polyester stuffing*

HobbyCraft Stores
Tel: 01452 424999
www.hobbycraft.co.uk
*All craft materials including beads (stores
throughout UK)*

John Lewis
Tel: 08456 049 049
www.johnlewis.com
*For fabric, threads, ribbons, trimmings,
beads, haberdashery (stores throughout UK)*

Paperchase
www.paperchase.co.uk
*For luggage tags, photo albums
(stores throughout UK)*

The Quilt Room
20 West Street, Dorking, Surrey RH4 1BL
Tel: 01306 877307
www.quiltroom.co.uk
Printed cottons and all quilting supplies

Sew and So
Stroud House, Russell Street, Stroud,
Glos GL5 3AN
Tel: 01453 889988
www.sewandso.co.uk
*For Just Another Button Company buttons,
coloured linen, threads, and various colours
of perforated paper. Buttons used in Heart
and Home Wreath: Tiny Ruth's Sparrow
button 1109.T; Tiny Sweet Heart Bird
button 1192.T; Tiny Raspberry Swirly Bud
button 2310.T; Tiny Rose buttons 2300.T;
Small Beehive button 1132.S*

Voirrey Embroidery Centre
Brimstage Hall, Brimstage, Wirral CH63 6JA
Tel: 0151 342 3514
www.voirrey.com
Embroidery and patchwork supplies

USA

Charles Craft Inc.
PO Box 1049, Laurenburg, NC 28353
Tel: 910 844 3521
www.charlescraft.com
*For fabrics for cross stitch and many useful
pre-finished items. (Coats Crafts UK supply
some Charles Craft products in the UK)*

The City Quilter
157 West 24th Street, New York, NY 1011
Tel: 212 807 0390
*For patchwork and quilting supplies (shop
and mail order)*

Joann Stores, Inc.
5555 Darrow Road, Hudson, Ohio
Tel: 1 888 739 4120
www.joann.com
*For general needlework and quilting
supplies (mail order and shops across US)*

MCG Textiles
13845 Magnolia Avenue, Chino, CA 91710
Tel: 909 591-6351
www.mcgtextiles.com
*For cross stitch fabrics and
pre-finished items*

M & J Buttons
1000 Sixth Avenue, New York, NY 10018
Tel: 212 391 6200
www.mjtrim.com
For beads, buttons, ribbons and trimmings

Mill Hill, a division of Wichelt Imports Inc.
N162 Hwy 35, Stoddard WI 54658
Tel: 608 788 4600
www.millhill.com
*For Mill Hill beads and a US source for
Framecraft products*

Acknowledgments

A big thank you to everyone at David & Charles for their skills, talent and hard work in producing this book. A special thank you to Cheryl Brown for commissioning another lovely book for me to create, and for all her brilliant ideas and inspirations. A special thank you, too, to Lin Clements who must be the most efficient project editor ever and is always a delight to work with. Thanks to Charley Bailey and Mia Farrant for the beautiful book design, to Bethany Dymond for all her help and to Simon Whitmore for the wonderful photography. Thank you to Cara Ackerman at DMC for providing all the beautiful threads I need. Finally, thank you to my husband and family for all their love and support.

About the Author

Helen Philipps studied printed textiles and embroidery at Manchester Metropolitan University and then taught drawing and design before becoming a freelance designer. After working in the greetings card industry, Helen's love of needlecraft lead her to create original designs for stitching magazines and her work is featured regularly in many cross stitch magazines. Helen's other books for David & Charles are: *The New Cross Stitch Sampler Book* (1999), *Helen Philipps' Cross Stitch Garden Notebook* (2001), *Cross Stitch Samplers and Cards* (2004) and *Quick & Clever Cross Stitch* (2006).

Index